Jon & Katherine,

Thank you for your faithful service to the body of Christ. Please pray that God will use this book to bless many young ladies!

NO TRESPASSING

Leah Holder Green

"OMG! *No Trespassing: I'm God's Property* has been such a blessing to my life. I promise the way I think and act have tremendously transformed—especially on what I listen to and what I allow myself to watch. *No Trespassing* has also allowed me to grow in my relationship with God, and I feel myself becoming closer and closer to Him every day. Thank you, Leah, for reaching out and sharing your testimony!"

—**Simone**, High School Student

"Reading *No Trespassing: I'm God's Property* is like having a heart-to-heart conversation with a close friend. In this book, I found advice, encouragement, and even a little reproof regarding things that I've taken too lightly. It is a book that I'll likely read again and again, just to keep reminding myself of my commitment to sexual purity and find encouragement for staying the course. I'm almost 27, and I've had my share of struggles, but I am in it to win it! Our bodies are temples of the Holy Spirit, and this book contains a message that this current generation really needs to hear. Stop reading this review and start reading this book if you haven't already!"

—**Divine**, Young Adult

"This book is absolutely wonderful! I want every girl to read it and be blessed by it. Leah Holder Green does such a great job of lovingly connecting truth about sexual purity into modern teenage vernacular. She provides sound logic and strong biblical application. She goes to the heart of sexual purity issues with such stark honesty and clarity that every teenager and adult can relate to and be benefited by this book. *No Trespassing: I'm God's Property* is a must-read for teenagers and young adult women!"

—**Dr. Mark Hartman**, Pastor

NO TRESPASSING
I'M *GOD'S* PROPERTY
Finally, the Truth About Sexual Purity

LEAH HOLDER GREEN

NASHVILLE

NEW YORK • LONDON • MELBOURNE • VANCOUVER

NO TRESPASSING
I'M *GOD'S* PROPERTY
Finally, the Truth About Sexual Purity

Published in New York, New York, by Morgan James Publishing. Morgan James is a trademark of Morgan James, LLC. www.MorganJamesPublishing.com

The Morgan James Speakers Group can bring authors to your live event. For more information or to book an event visit The Morgan James Speakers Group at www.TheMorganJamesSpeakersGroup.com.

Scripture taken from the Holy Bible, New International Version®, NIV® Copyright© 1973, 1978, 1984 by Biblica, Inc.™ Used by permission of Zondervan. All rights reserved worldwide. WWW.ZONDERVAN.COM

The "NIV" and "New International Version" are trademarks registered in the United States Patent and Trademark Offices by Biblica, Inc.

ISBN 978-1-63047-369-3 paperback
ISBN 978-1-63047-370-9 eBook
ISBN 978-1-63047-371-6 hardcover
Library of Congress Control Number: 2014945793

Original Cover Concept by:
Jacque Sellers

Cover Design by:
Rachel Lopez
www.r2cdesign.com

Interior Design by:
Bonnie Bushman
bonnie@caboodlegraphics.com

In an effort to support local communities, raise awareness and funds, Morgan James Publishing donates a percentage of all book sales for the life of each book to Habitat for Humanity Peninsula and Greater Williamsburg.

Get involved today! Visit
www.MorganJamesBuilds.com

DEDICATION

For my sister, Janelle Nikole Holder. Your time on this earth was short, and I believe the Lord has given me a double portion of blessings and favor—both yours and mine. I aim to live a life that pleases Him and makes you proud of your little sister.

TABLE OF CONTENTS

FOREWORD

I am excited about Leah Holder Green, her cutting-edge ministry, and her book, *No Trespassing: I'm God's Property*. This book is a must-read for young ladies and parents alike.

In this book, Leah certainly does not try to take a parent's role. Rather, she shares her personal experiences and the reasons why she chooses to remain sexually pure. By reading *No Trespassing*, young ladies will gain knowledge on how to escape the temptations of the world today, and parents will have a better understanding of what their daughters face on a daily basis. Leah writes as clearly and concisely as she speaks, getting both into your mind and your spirit, and leaving you with an impact that will touch you to the core of your being.

As Leah's pastor, I am honored to write this foreword on her behalf. My prayer is that *No Trespassing: I'm God's Property* will encourage you to evaluate your lifestyle and help you realize who you really belong to.

—**Michael A. Pender, Sr.**, Senior Pastor
Fallbrook Church, Houston, Texas

ACKNOWLEDGEMENTS

I must first thank the One who called, anointed, and equipped me to write this book, my Lord and Savior, Jesus Christ. All the glory and all the honor go to You.

To my amazing family—Mom, Daddy "O," Grandma Josie, Grandmommy, and Jahgee. Mom, thank you for the unconditional love and affirmation of my worth you've given me throughout my life. You are my best friend. Daddy "O," thank you for your continual encouragement and for always making me feel as though I truly am *the apple of your eye.* I'm so grateful God entrusted me to your loving care. Grandma Josie, thank you so much for always reminding me how blessed I am and for constantly telling me to "keep looking up." Grandmommy, thank you for your priceless involvement in my life. Because of you, I always know that someone is praying for me and that someone deeply loves me. Jahgee, thank you for constantly telling me how proud of me you are. You are one of the most incredible men I know, and your support means the world to me. All of you loved and believed in me long before I ever loved or believed in myself. With all my heart, I appreciate you. With all my heart, I love you.

To the shepherd of Fallbrook Church, Pastor Mike. Thank you for leading your family and our church with integrity. My love and respect for you and Sis. Jan are far greater than you may ever know. Thank you for your contribution to and support of me and this project.

To the two people who sparked the beginning of this project and saw it through until the end, Dr. Stephen Trammell and Laura Gallier. Dr. Trammell, as I entered your office that day, I had no idea I would leave with a plan to compose my first book. You helped confirm to me that God is ordering my steps, and I am abundantly grateful that He led me to someone as Christ-like and genuine as you. Laura, what an inspiration you are to me. Thank you for sacrificing your time to pour wisdom and knowledge into me. I can't imagine what this book would be without you two. So, from the bottom of my heart, thank you.

To Kelly Cowthran, thank you for all of your invaluable input in the editing and promotion of this project. You are remarkable, and I'm honored to call you my friend.

To all of those who gave me feedback and supported this project, Dr. Mark Hartman, Dr. Jim Richards, Jim Broadhead, Lawren Robertson, Sheila Miller, Darlene Carter, Jessica Trevino, Erica Giwa, Jennifer Green, Shevonne Hemphill, and Tonya Trammell, thank you, thank you, thank you!

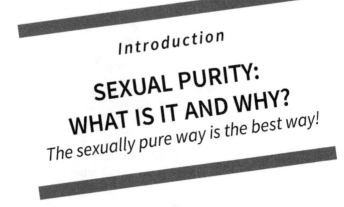

Introduction

SEXUAL PURITY: WHAT IS IT AND WHY?

The sexually pure way is the best way!

"It is God's will that you should be sanctified [pure]:
that you should avoid sexual immorality."
1 Thessalonians 4:3

Why Should We Be Sexually Pure?

When I was 17 years old, I liked to hang out with the other teenagers in my neighborhood. We would talk for hours, and I enjoyed our conversations. Yet one day, my conversation with one of the guys made me feel uncomfortable. He kept making comments about us having sex in the near future. I finally stopped him and said, "I'm not having sex with you." "What's wrong with me?" he responded. I gave it to him straight saying, "I'm not having sex with anyone before marriage. I want to be sexually pure." This guy looked at me as though I was an alien from outer space, and then he asked me a short but loaded question. "Why?"

Even now, people ask me basically the same question about my commitment to sexual purity—*why? Why should anyone live sexually pure?* Maybe you're asking yourself that question right now. So before I dive into *how* you and I can live sexually pure, let's discuss *why* we should.

Sexual Impurity Has a High Cost

Many young women, including some Christian women, fall into the trap of sexual impurity. The consequence is brokenness—broken hearts, broken lives, broken families, and broken fellowship with God. Even non-religious studies show that people who engage in sexual activity outside of marriage have higher rates of sexually transmitted diseases, unwanted pregnancies, divorce, and a number of emotional problems. It's true that we all fail at something at some point, but I once heard Pastor Andy Stanley explain why failing to live sexually pure is different than failing in other areas of our lives. He pointed out how we can fully recover from many other kinds of failures.

For example, financially, you and I could lose all of our money at one point, and later on become millionaires. Educationally, you and I could drop out of school at one time, and then later earn GEDs, Masters degrees, and Doctorate degrees. Professionally, you and I could get fired at one point, and later on become presidents or CEOs. However, sexual purity failures cause more devastating consequences in our lives, often resulting in irreversible damage. Sexual purity failures can cause wounds that no amount of money, no degree, and no accomplishment can heal.

God's Way is The Best Way

God created sex, and He does want us to enjoy it. But He wants us to enjoy it within His boundaries. His boundary for sex is marriage, period. *But what if my boyfriend and I really love each other?* Nope. *But what if we're going to get married one day?* Nope. *But what if that's the only way this guy will stay with me?* Certainly not, and that guy is not the one for you anyway. God intended sex to be enjoyed within one man and one woman's marital covenant. Is that because God wants to ruin our fun? Not at all!

God wants us to stay within His boundaries for the same reason my grandma wanted my dad and his brothers to stay inside the fence around their house. "Don't y'all go out there!" she would warn them. My dad grew up in a gang-infested area on the south side of Chicago. The other side of the fence seemed fun to him and his brothers, but my grandma could see things that they couldn't. She could see the harm and danger awaiting them on the other side of that fence, and she wanted to protect her children.

This world makes sex outside of marriage look so glamorous in all the movies, TV shows, and music videos. Like my dad and uncles, you and I may think the world's side of the fence looks fun. But like my grandma, God can see things that we can't. He knows the harm and danger that await us if we have sex the world's way, and He wants to protect us, His children.

In the "Guardrails" chapter of this book, we will discuss God's protection in greater detail. The main point I want you to get right now is this: You and I should be sexually pure, because doing so allows us to stay within God's protection. And when we step outside of God's protection, we get hurt. We should follow God's plan, because His way is the best way.

Bound to be Free

If you're a Christian, you should live sexually pure not only to avoid harm but also to honor God and experience true freedom. Many people associate God's boundaries with bondage. The reality is that the complete opposite is true: God's will is actually the most liberating and satisfying place to be. It wasn't until I truly pursued purity—in mind, body, and heart—that I experienced a new level of intimacy and peace with God. After this experience, I never wanted to go back to the way I used to live! Living sexually pure isn't about exercising our willpower, feeling better about ourselves, or any other self-centered reason. It's about loving God and honoring Him with holy lives. It's about giving all of ourselves to the One who gave us all of Himself.

What is Sexual Purity Anyway?

Throughout this book, I will use the phrase *sexually pure*. I'll define what it means now. If you and I are sexually pure, that means we do not provoke or please our sexual desires outside of God's will. In other words, we do not read, watch, listen to, or do things that will stir up our sexual desires. Even more importantly, we don't do anything that will satisfy our sexual desires. As we briefly discussed, God's will for sex is that we enjoy it only within marriage.

Because this book is intended primarily for singles, I will address sexual purity from that perspective. Sexual purity applies to married people too. However, married people can satisfy *some* sexual desires within God's will, but singles cannot. *No fair*, you may be thinking. By the time you finish this book, I hope you will see the beauty of God's plan, and that His way is much better than the world's way.

Should You Read This Book?

If you are a young lady, a parent, or both, I encourage you to read this book. You can benefit from reading it, regardless of where you are in your life right now—whether you're a virgin or not, whether you're currently living sexually pure or not. If you're a parent with daughters, your daughters either have experienced, are experiencing, or will experience the sexual pressures of this world. Reading this book could help you help them.

Throughout the book, I discuss sexual purity within the context of opposite-sex relations. However, if you have same-sex attractions and sexual interactions, I encourage you to read it anyway. There are many different ways to be sexually impure, but the same God can set all of us free. The principles in this book can lead you to His freedom, so I pray you will join me on this journey. I also recommend that you look into the testimony of a poet named Jackie Hill Perry.

Because my convictions are based on my relationship with Jesus Christ, biblical principles provide the foundation for this book. If you are not a Christian, I encourage you to read it anyway. You have nothing to lose and everything to gain.

I Want to Encourage You

With this book, I hope to help you embrace a lifestyle of sexual purity. If you are not living sexually pure right now, I pray this book will show you that God still loves you. I hope He will use it to lead you to a life of sexual purity. If you are already on the sexually pure path, I pray this book will encourage you to stay on it.

I have struggled with sexual purity, but I find victory through Christ Jesus. The Lord has given me a passion to encourage you, and He has blessed me with a beautiful testimony to share with you. By His grace, I am a virgin who has not even kissed a guy. In addition to learning more of my testimony in this book, you will get biblical truths, personal experiences, and practical tips to help equip you for your sexual purity journey. To get the most out of this book, I suggest reading it more than once and taking time to answer the Reflection Questions.

No Trespassing

I have lived in Texas since I was seven years old, and I possess my fair share of Texas pride. In addition to football and big stuff, we Texans take pride in our private property. It is common to see signs that read "NO TRESPASSING." In fact, owners can legally shoot anyone who does trespass on their land. I told you, we value our property down here.

God carefully created you in your mother's womb (Psalm 139:13). You are His precious masterpiece. You are His private property (1 Corinthians 6:19-20). As you begin or continue your sexual purity journey, I encourage you to tell all sexual impurity *NO TRESPASSING—No trespassing in my mind, no trespassing on my body, and no trespassing in my heart.* Thank you for joining me on this journey, my friend. Let's dig in!

Reflection Question:

Based on the definition of sexual purity provided in this Introduction, do you consider yourself sexually pure at this time? Why or why not?

Prayer Starter:

Dear God,

Thank You for loving me and having a good plan for my life. Since there are no accidents, I know You brought this book into my life for a reason. Please help me hear clearly everything You will say to me through this book. And please let my life be more pleasing to You after reading it. In Jesus' name, Amen.

Section One

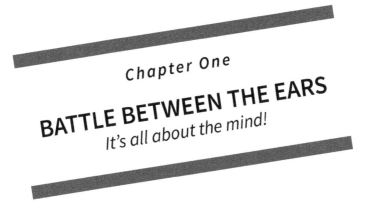

Chapter One
BATTLE BETWEEN THE EARS
It's all about the mind!

"But we have the mind of Christ."
1 Corinthians 2:16b

Y ou and I should live sexually pure, because that's the best way to live. It allows us to stay in God's will, which is the safest and most satisfying place to be. I tell you these facts with the highest confidence. What I won't tell you is that living sexually pure is easy. I won't tell you that, because it isn't true. In fact, living sexually pure can be quite difficult at times, because we have to battle within our own minds.

Our sexual purity, or the lack thereof, begins in our minds, period. We have thousands of thoughts every day. Naturally, some of those thoughts may try to wander into sexually impure places. Trying to keep

3

our thoughts out of those places is indeed a battle! Let's see why fighting for purity in our minds is so important.

Control Them, or They'll Control You

Have you ever seen a person walking a big dog, but it appears the big dog is actually walking the person? I can just imagine the dog telling its owner, "If you don't control me, I will control you!" In that respect, our thoughts are a lot like big dogs. If we don't work to control our thoughts, they will certainly control us. It is impossible, I repeat, *impossible* to live sexually pure, if we have no control over our minds.

I didn't always believe this reality, though. When I was a teen, I just couldn't understand how it could be bad to only *think about stuff.* Why was it wrong to only think about being mean to someone who upset me? I didn't actually do it, so there was no harm done, right? In regards to sexual purity, why was it wrong to only think about making out with or even going all the way with a cute guy? Surely, that was better than actually *doing* it, right?

Then one day, I came across a verse in the Bible that burst my bubble. The first part of Proverbs 23:7 says, "For as [she] thinketh in [her] heart, so is [she]…" Basically, the verse declares that we are what we think. Wow! So much for *harmless* fantasies, huh? The way we consistently think determines who we are; the sum total of our thoughts reveals the real us.

Don't we see this truth at play in other contexts? If someone consistently thinks depressing thoughts, won't she be a depressed person? If someone consistently thinks negative thoughts, won't she be a negative person? It's no different with thoughts regarding sexual purity. If you and I consistently think sexually impure thoughts, we will be sexually impure people.

Thoughts, especially sexually impure ones, are not like stagnant puddles of water that eventually evaporate. Instead, they are like cancers that if not removed or addressed, will grow, spread, and worsen over time. If we allow these thoughts to go unchecked, they will consume our entire bodies and our entire lives. We will reach a point where we feel as though we *must* obey or act out those thoughts.

I began to realize that I had it all wrong. My thought life was actually very important to my sexual purity. I believed that by only thinking sexual thoughts, I was resting comfortably on some middle ground. I had a rude awakening when I discovered that no middle ground exists.

Either we control our thoughts, or our thoughts control us—end of story. I decided I could not be an example of sexually pure living, if I did not get control of my thoughts. In this battle for my mind, I would no longer allow my impure thoughts to beat me up. I had to fight for my mind. I encourage you to fight for yours too!

We Can't Help It, But We Can

Think about where you live right now. Do you have complete control over who comes to your door and knocks on it? You may live in a house, apartment, or dorm in a nice area of town. In fact, you or your family may have moved there specifically because of its security measures, such as security gates, security guards, and surveillance cameras. Even so, it's possible that someone could get around those security measures and knock on your door. Can you control that? Of course not.

However, once that person knocks on your door, do you have to invite him in and let him stay a while? Certainly not! You have options. If you don't recognize him, you can ask him to state his name and his purpose for knocking on your door. If his responses don't satisfy you, or if you think he's up to no good, you can tell him to leave. Depending on his response, you can take the necessary and *legal* steps to make sure he does leave.

What in the world does that have to do with sexual thoughts in our minds? Well, as with our homes' doors, we do not have complete control over what thoughts knock on our minds' doors. We all have mental battles, because for the most part, we all have sexual desires and thoughts. God created us, and God created sex. Because He created us as sexual beings, some of those desires and thoughts are natural, not inherently sinful.

Being aware of this fact helps us better understand ourselves and our makeup. When we understand our makeup, we can avoid becoming overly confident in ourselves and overly critical of ourselves. It's true, we cannot control the onset of every sexual urge or sexual thought that comes to our minds. However, we can control the way we respond to those urges and thoughts. Just as we don't have to invite everyone who knocks to stay in our homes, we don't have to allow every thought that knocks to stay in our minds.

Let's apply these principles to a real-life situation. Imagine an athletically-built, good-looking, shirtless man runs by you and me in the park. (Don't imagine too hard!) Oh. My. Goodness. We may not be able to control the thought that knocks at our minds' doors as that guy passes before our eyes. Even if we've established some mental security measures, like studying the Bible and praying, that thought may sneak up and knock anyway.

Do we have to invite that thought in and let it stay a while? No! And unlike with the stranger at our door, we don't need to ask the thought to state its name or its purpose, because we already know: Its name is Lust, and its purpose is to consume us. We can skip right to the part where we tell that thought to leave. Then, we do whatever it takes to make sure it does leave.

In summary, we cannot always control the onset of sexual urges or thoughts that arise within us, but we can control our responses to them. Allowing those sinful urges and thoughts to stay around is the wrong response. What's the right one? It's responding to those urges and thoughts, as we would to dangerous visitors at our doors—demanding that they leave and not resting until they do!

Let's Fight

Sometimes, it may not feel like those sexual thoughts simply knock at our minds' doors. Instead, it may feel as though they pound and kick. This is when the fighting commences. We must fight back. I define "fighting" as resisting and wrestling with those thoughts, as opposed to allowing them to run freely in our minds.

There is a big difference between resisting sin and downright practicing it. The initial look or thought about a guy is natural, and then we must resist the temptation to let it stay. If we allow that look or thought to linger, it will grow into a strong sexual desire and longing for that person. In other words, it will grow into lust.

Because resisting lust conflicts with our sinful nature, it does require hard work. Once we accept Christ as our Lord and Savior, we receive the Holy Spirit (John 14:15-18). At this point, our Spirit nature takes root. Yet, we were born with our sinful nature, and it doesn't disappear once we get the Spirit nature. So do you see why we have a battle going on within us?

We have two distinct natures pulling us in two distinct directions (Romans 7:21-25). Our two natures will battle until we go to Heaven, but we can experience victory here on earth. Our sinful nature has this advantage: We were born with it, so it doesn't require much effort to obey it. Think about it, did anyone sit down and teach you how to lie? Most likely not. You probably know how to do it, though. Likewise, we aren't *taught* how to lust, but we sure know how to do it. As my dad often says, we are "naughty by nature."

As true as that is, our Spirit nature has a greater advantage: It holds the power of God! It is His power that can give us victory over sin now.

However, we can't passively sit around and wait for the Lord to deliver us. We have a role to play too. We must fight, and we must resist. If our sinful nature hits us with lust, our Spirit nature must hit back. What can our Spirit nature use to fight back? The Bible is the best weapon.

If those lustful thoughts keep attacking us, and we feel as though we just can't take any more hits, we can hit them back with 1 Corinthians 10:13, which says, "No temptation has seized you except what is common to man. And God is faithful; he will not let you be tempted beyond what you can bear. But when you are tempted, he will also provide a way out so that you can stand up under it."

It's true, this battling can become tiring, and we may feel like just giving in. *This is too hard,* we say to ourselves. We may even think that no one could ever resist the mental temptations we're facing. Yet 1 Corinthians 10:13 tells us that our temptations are nothing new. Many people before us struggled with them and won, and many people after us will struggle with them and win. If they can do it, we can too.

The Scripture also promises that whenever we're tempted, God will "provide a way out." When people say they didn't see a way out of a bad situation, that doesn't mean there was no way out. That means they did not look for a way out. When you and I are tempted to let our minds go to sexually impure places, we must look for God's escape route. The exit will be there, and we must find it and use it.

Get Busy and Stay Busy

When I was in college, I noticed a pattern in my mental purity. During school, my thought life usually got better. Yet in the summertime, my thought life always got worse. I used to wonder, *What is it about coming home in the summer that causes me to struggle so much more?* I think there were a few reasons, but here's the main one: A bored mind will usually become an impure mind.

As we discussed, God will always give us a way out of sexual temptations. That's great, but you and I can avoid many temptations simply by staying busy. Why depend on escaping from a trap, if you can avoid the trap altogether? I have five words for you, my friend: Get busy and stay busy.

If you're in school, study as hard as you can. Do all your homework and the extra credit, too! When you finish that, get involved in some extracurricular activities—sports, drama, choir, debate, or anything you enjoy. Do whatever it takes to get busy and stay busy.

If you're a working adult, work as hard as you can on your job. If you finish and have nothing else to do, put in some overtime! You can also get involved in a ministry at your church, volunteer at your local nursing home, coach a children's soccer team, join a fitness class, learn to play an instrument, or do anything you enjoy. Whatever you do, just make sure you get busy and stay busy.

Even at this point in my sexual purity journey, my thoughts do better when I get and stay busy. I recently had a few days off of work, and guess what? I struggled much more than I usually do. Why? I wasn't busy enough. So in this fight for our minds, we now know a very important battle tactic—get busy and stay busy.

Your Thoughts Are Showing

Do our thoughts affect only our minds? No. Our thoughts have a greater impact on our physical realities than we tend to realize. As I mentioned, I certainly did not recognize the influence of my thoughts when I was younger. However, over time, I learned that all sinful actions begin as sinful thoughts. Before we do anything, we think about it. Even when people say, "I acted without thinking," what they're truly saying is that they didn't think *carefully* enough about their actions and the possible consequences. Whether they realize it or not, they did think about it before they did it. This is the *thought-life domino effect*: If we don't fight for our minds, our thoughts will spiral out of control; if our thoughts are out of control, they begin to show up in our actions.

For instance, allowing sexually graphic images to run freely in our minds will lead to their manifestation in our physical lives. For some, it may lead to masturbation or ways of privately satisfying sexual arousals. For others, it may lead to more sexual contact with partners, ranging from heavy kissing and touching to full-blown sexual intercourse. Regardless of the specifics, this underlying truth remains: A sexually impure mind leads to a sexually impure body.

This truth is why we must fight in our minds' battles against impurity. If we don't take hold of those impure thoughts, they will take us to deep, dark places we never intended to go. I repeat, if we don't control our thoughts, they will control us. There is no middle ground!

In It to Win It

I played basketball in high school. Since my dad was a basketball star in his day, I would often talk to him about upcoming games. One day, I told him my team thought we were going to lose our next game, because our opponents were bigger and quicker than us. I quickly regretted telling him that, because he became quite upset.

He said if my team and I entered the game with a defeated attitude, we had already lost the game. He sternly said, "Leah, there's no reason to play in a game you expect to lose. If you're going to be in it, you must be in it to win it." This valuable lesson impacted me, not only in basketball games but also in other areas of my life. Yes, even my sexual purity journey.

We must not only fight against sexual impurity, but we must fight to win. Let's not enter our battles with "the body is weak" attitude. People are so quick to quote that part of the Scripture, but I don't hear nearly as many people quote the preceding part, which says, "Watch and pray so that you will not fall into temptation" (Matthew 26:41).

Watching and praying pack a powerful one-two punch in our fight against sexual impurity. We watch out for potential dangers, like seductive guys, perverse music, and explicit movies or books. (We'll discuss these dangers in greater detail in the next chapter.) Then we pray to the Lord for wisdom to perceive the dangers and for strength to withstand them.

These efforts are vital, because if we habitually lose our battles, we will delay our progress and our spiritual growth. Each loss will discourage us and dig a deeper hole for us. We will become more susceptible to the lies that *we just can't do it* and *we're too far gone.* Conversely, each win gives us more strength and more resolve to win the next one.

Got Power?

You may be thinking, *I don't think I can win these battles on my own.* If so, you are exactly right. We cannot win on our own. But with the Lord's help, we certainly can! In 2 Corinthians 12:9, God says that His power is perfected in our weakness. In essence, God assures us that our weaknesses provide the perfect conditions for Him to display His great power in our lives.

One day as I typed on my laptop, I noticed my battery's charge was getting low. I grabbed the end of my charger, plugged it into my laptop, and continued to type. A few minutes later, I noticed that my battery's charge was even lower than it was earlier! That's when I discovered the other end of my charger was not plugged into the outlet. Once I plugged my charger into the outlet, it could finally experience the electric power from that outlet.

By ourselves, we don't have power. But God's got the power. He's the source of our strength. All we have to do is *plug into* Him, and we'll witness Him do amazing things. How do we plug into God's power and strength? I'm so glad you asked!

- We read and study His book, the Bible (Joshua 1:8).
- We pray continually (1 Thessalonians 5:17).
- We follow His leading by the Holy Spirit (John 16:13).

Bible study, prayer, and the Holy Spirit allow us to plug into God's power. If we don't use them, we'll be like my laptop's battery—go unchanged and gradually get worse. When we do use them, we'll be empowered, and we'll win battles against impurity with increasing consistency. When other temptations arise, we will recall how God helped us withstand the last one. This will make us more determined to win and not give in.

The more we've tasted victory, the more we have to lose if we fail. This, too, can increase our resolve *not* to fail. At one point in my life, for about six months, I did well winning my mental battles against impurity. Then, one day, I lost a mental battle. I just stopped fighting momentarily. *No big deal,* I thought to myself. But that one defeat led me into a mental losing streak for a while.

Then, I repented to the Lord and started over. About six months later, I encountered a strong temptation to give in again. I thought back to the last time when that *one* loss led me into a losing streak. So this time, I dug in deep and surrendered to the Lord. I said, "Lord, I refuse to go back to losing my mental battles. I can't do it alone, though. I need Your help." The result was nothing short of a miracle. The Lord did help me win, and He continues to help me win. And guess what, my friend? He will help you win too.

Because He Said So

Have you ever asked your parents the question *why?* I once heard a little boy repeatedly asking his mother that question in the grocery store. Every time he asked to get something, she would refuse, and then he would whine, "But why, mommy?" After the fourth time, the woman turned to her son and firmly said, "Because I said so." To my delight, that little boy quickly stopped whining and asking why.

The most important reason we must fight to win our mental battles against impurity is because God has called us to do so. As with that little boy and his mom in the grocery store, we should do what God says simply because He says so. The bottom line is this: Losing our mental battles is sin in the eyes of God. He sees and judges our thoughts.

I came across another verse in the Bible that transformed my theory on thoughts, especially in regards to lustful thoughts. Matthew 5:28 reads, "But I tell you that anyone who looks at a [man] lustfully has already committed adultery with [him] in [her] heart." Basically, God says that if we envision sleeping with a guy, in His eyes, we actually did sleep with that guy. Once again, so much for *innocent* fantasies! I realized that since God is the only one who can see my thoughts, He is the only one who can rightfully deem me to be sexually pure or impure. If I want Him to view me as sexually pure, I have to win my mental battles against lust.

It's simple: If we don't win, we sin. This reality should not be taken lightly, because habitual, unrepentant sin can lead to sinful strongholds. Unchecked sinful strongholds can lead to our destruction and death. Perhaps they won't lead to an immediate physical death, but they may lead to a spiritual one.

I know, that sounds depressing. You may be thinking, *I thought this book was supposed to encourage me!* Well, here's your encouragement: God doesn't call us to do anything without equipping us to do it. Since He has called us to be sexually pure, He will supply us with what we need to do so.

Remember that promise we read in 1 Corinthians 10:13, "No temptation has seized you except what is common to man. And God is faithful; *he will not let you be tempted beyond what you can bear. But when you are tempted, he will also provide a way out so that you can stand up under it.*" This Scripture assures us that we can win our mental battles against sexual impurity. If we actually seek God's help, we will win.

In the next chapter, we will discuss how we can help ourselves win our battles. It's true, we must plug into God's strength through prayer, Bible study, and obedience to the Holy Spirit. At the same time, there are practical steps we can take to stop some lustful thoughts before they begin. So please continue with me on this journey!

Reflection Questions:

If your thoughts were displayed on a public, big screen, would you be ashamed of anything? Explain.

Is it more accurate to say that you control your thoughts, or that your thoughts control you? If your thoughts control you, what impact is that having on your life?

List three benefits you see to having a more disciplined thought life.

Prayer Starter:

Dear God,

I'm so thankful that You know the battles I face in my mind. I'm even more thankful that You can and will help me be victorious in those battles. Remind me that I can always turn to You, especially when I feel weak. In Jesus' name, Amen.

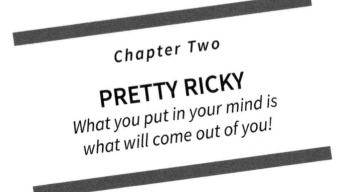

Chapter Two

PRETTY RICKY
What you put in your mind is what will come out of you!

*"Do not be deceived: God cannot be mocked.
A man [woman] reaps what he [she] sows."*
Galatians 6:7

W e've established that there are battles going on in our minds, and that in order to be sexually pure, we must fight and win those battles. Now for the million-dollar question: How do we prepare ourselves to fight and win those mental battles against lust? Well, one of the best ways to answer that question is to first answer this one: How do we prepare ourselves to *lose* these mental battles?

A Lesson from Ketchup

Imagine that you completely fill a bottle with ketchup. Upon squeezing that bottle, would you expect mustard to come out? Of course not.

Why? Because whatever you fill a container with is what will come out when you squeeze it.

This principle applies to us as well. We are the containers, and through our ears and eyes, we are filled with images and ideas. If we fill ourselves with sexually explicit, lustful material, what should we expect to come out when we are *squeezed* or tempted? We certainly shouldn't expect to see self-control or holiness, should we? No, that would be like expecting mustard from a bottle of ketchup. You and I shouldn't fill ourselves with trash and expect to see triumph, with perversion and expect to see purity. What we put in our minds is indeed what will come out of us.

When people ask me to share my testimony about being a virgin, I share it quickly and unashamedly. However, I'm equally quick to share that even though I am a virgin, I have not always been sexually pure. There were times when I filled my mind with impurity. How exactly did I do that? The two main sources were music and television.

Please DO Stop the Music

Do you like music? I *love* music. I can listen to and enjoy just about any genre. Put on some good, bass-heavy music, and you will see my usually laid-back demeanor fade away, as I begin to nod my head and bounce my shoulders. Put on some good, soft music, and you will see my eyes close, my head recline, and a warm smile appear on my face, while I gently sway from side to side. Yeah, music moves me. This may seem innocent, and in some cases, it is innocent. However, the wrong type of music can and has moved me in the wrong direction.

When I was in high school, there was a popular boy band out called Pretty Ricky. One of my classmates at school gave me a copy of Pretty Ricky's CD. He said my parents would never allow me to buy it myself. When I listened to the CD that night, I understood what he meant! That

CD had some of the most sexually graphic lyrics and sensual melodies I had ever heard in my life.

Even though I knew it was inappropriate, I was undeniably intrigued by it. The lead vocalist had a smooth voice, and the melodies were pleasing to my ears. Even though the lyrics made me uncomfortable at first, the more I listened, the less they bothered me. I really didn't think listening to this music was a big deal or that it could significantly affect me. I was wrong.

I began to notice certain curiosities and desires arising within me that weren't there before. The songs' lyrics and my own sinful nature were a dynamic duo; they teamed up to create images in my mind that remained with me long after I turned off the music. Did you catch that? That sensual, sexually explicit music stirred up lustful thoughts and lustful desires within me that *weren't* there before.

In my battle against lust, I provided the enemy with ammunition and then left myself exposed to its attack. What kind of battle tactic was that? It was a battle tactic that ensured I lost, that's what! If you and I truly want to fight and win our battles against lust, we cannot listen to music that encourages it. Our musical selection and our desire for sexual purity must align with one another.

Best Buys

During a youth Bible study one night, I began to feel guilty about listening to Pretty Ricky's CD and other inappropriate songs. I confessed to the Bible study group that I knew I shouldn't listen to such music, and that I knew I should delete all of it from my iTunes library. I also confessed that I didn't like the thought of deleting items from my iTunes library. That's when the youth pastor suggested that I not only delete negative items but also replace them with positive alternatives.

To be honest, I wasn't sure there were any *quality* positive alternatives. I wasn't aware of any high-quality, Christian music in genres I liked. So,

I was stunned when I found Christian artists who were just as musically gifted as secular artists. I discovered an abundance of outstanding Christian music in an assortment of genres. For Rock/Pop lovers, there's Hillsong United, Unspoken, Casting Crowns, and many, many others. For Hip-Hop lovers, there's Lecrae, Andy Mineo, Flame, and a host of others. If you like it all, you'd probably enjoy Israel Houghton, Jamie Grace, Mandisa, or TobyMac, because they do it all.

The examples I've mentioned don't even scratch the surface of positive musical alternatives. I hope this assures you that you don't have to listen to boring, poor-quality music in order to remain pure. We shouldn't close the door to negative music and then cry over what we've lost. Instead, we should open the door to exceptional positive music and be grateful for what we've gained.

Does this mean we can never listen to any secular music? Not necessarily. I'm specifically referring to secular music that contains sexual innuendos and sexually explicit content. When deciding whether to listen to other kinds of secular music, we must use our own judgment. In order to protect myself, I've decided to steer clear of most secular music, especially when it contains content contrary to God's Word.

However, is it possible you may occasionally find me listening to (and *attempting* to sing along with) Whitney Houston's "I Will Always Love You"? Absolutely! I don't suggest we become legalistic about our music choices and live under a rock. Rather, I do suggest we become selective about our music choices and live under God's covering.

Watch Out for What You Watch

If I had to rank my favorite entertainment choices, music would get first place. Movies and TV shows would get a close second place, though. If I had a dollar for every movie and TV show episode I've seen, I could retire right now. How about you? I've seen and enjoyed movies of all kinds—old, new, comedy, romance, suspense, drama, science fiction, you name it. I can even watch the same movie over and over again. The same is true for television shows. I've seen and enjoyed a wide range of them.

As with my love for music, my love for movies and TV, in itself, is innocent. However, many of the movies and some of the sitcoms I've seen are not. In fact, most of the newer movies and sitcoms out now are far from innocent.

Frog Legs

I have found great danger in watching the sexually impure images many of these movies and TV programs portray. To get a clearer picture of this danger, let's talk about cooking frog legs. Do you know how to cook frog legs? I'm no expert at it myself, but I once heard an old man from West Texas explain how he makes them.

He said that the frogs are actually alive when he puts them on the stove. They sit cozily in a pot partially filled with room-temperature water. He lets the frogs sit there for a little while, and then he, ever so slightly, turns up the heat under the stove burner. He waits a few more minutes and then gently turns up the heat a bit more. This process continues until, lo and behold, those formerly live frogs become cooked frogs. And that's how you get frog legs.

What do you think about that? At any given moment, with all that power in their hind legs, those frogs could have easily leaped out of that pot. And if the old man had tried to put them in boiling water, they certainly would have done so. Yet, because he gradually turned up the heat, the frogs gradually adjusted to the water's increasing temperature. They did not realize what was happening. They did not know their lives were slipping away.

Similarly, you and I can unknowingly let our purity slip away. Most likely, we will quickly jump out of the world's pot when we see something explicitly sexually impure. But what about the more subtle, less obvious forms of sexual perversion? You know, a music video that glamorizes premarital sex, a movie that promotes adultery, a sitcom that condones homosexuality, and so on. Could it really be wrong, when they make it look so beautiful or amusing? Yes, it's wrong!

With each movie, episode, and video of this sort we intake, the temperature on our stoves increases. If we're not careful, we will become just like those frogs. We'll become more and more desensitized to the perversion, until we find ourselves cooked by the culture, unable to distinguish between God's truth and the culture's opinions.

Eye Exam

I had to make up in my mind that I refuse to be cooked by this decadent culture. And one way I protect myself from being cooked is by protecting my eyes. The condition of our eyes is important to Jesus. In Matthew 6:22-23, Jesus says, "The eye is the lamp of the body. If your eyes are good, your whole body will be full of light. But if your eyes are bad, your whole body will be full of darkness..."

So, how's your eye health? If you don't know, give yourself an "eye exam" by taking inventory of what you watch. Then you'll have your answer. Guarding our eyes is difficult, and I don't profess to have it all figured out. Even so, I put great effort into guarding myself against movies and sitcoms I believe will have a negative effect on my purity. I encourage you to do the same.

Am I saying you shouldn't like movies anymore? Not at all, my friend. I still love movies. I have just become much more selective about which ones I will allow myself to view. I hardly watch any new television shows, and I practically never surf through the cable channels. (That has gotten me in big "purity trouble" before!) I tend to DVR old classic television sitcoms, movies I've already seen, various sports, and even some cartoons. I'm not ashamed to admit I'm a young adult who still watches cartoons! When I sit down in front of the TV, I go straight to the Recordings Menu, select one, and watch it while I eat or do whatever I'm doing. Will you consider developing a similar routine?

By Any Means Necessary

Some people may say my approach is lame, boring, or conversely, *a bit much*. My response to them would be, "Maybe for you it is, but for me, it's what I need to stay on track." In Mark 9:47, Jesus says, "And if your eye causes you to sin, pluck it out. It is better for you to enter the kingdom of God with one eye than to have two eyes and be thrown into hell." Whoa, that's intense!

Did Jesus mean we should literally pluck out our eyes, so we don't fall into sin? I don't think so. I do think He meant we should avoid sin by any means necessary—no matter how lame or radical those means may seem. In my case, it's better to watch shows and movies I know are safe for me.

You may decide to discontinue the cable on your television or to stop going to the movies. Then again, you may be able to handle movies and shows that would cause many others to stumble. Our routines may be different, but the key is to be honest with ourselves. If we think there is even the slightest chance a movie or show may hinder our sexual purity, we should leave it alone.

Will we be perfect at making these purity judgments? No. But we'll get better at making them as we grow in maturity and knowledge of ourselves. We'll see some commercial or movie preview and our "sexual purity alarms" will sound off, signaling us to retreat!

The "P" Word

One night, I watched the end of a PG movie on digital cable. The movie was a clean comedy I'd watched several times in the past. On this particular night, though, I wasn't exactly watching the movie. I was typing a Facebook note, and the movie acted as background noise.

Perhaps it was for this reason I let all the ending credits conclude without flipping the channel or turning off the TV. Before I was fully aware of it, the next movie began.

I glanced up and saw various women dressed in skimpy clothes and walking on a catwalk. I shook my head with slight disapproval but assumed it was a movie about runway modeling. So, I went back to typing. But I was mistaken. Before the opening credits were even finished, an explicit sexual scene unfolded on the TV screen. This was a downright pornographic movie.

After being momentarily paralyzed by utter shock and horror, I began frantically searching and fumbling for the remote. I flipped the channel, turned off the television, and sat stunned for a moment. Although it felt like slow motion, the whole ordeal took place in a matter of about five seconds. The images instantly disappeared from the television screen, but they did not instantly disappear from my mind.

I grappled with those images in my mind, fighting to suppress and beat them into holy submission. I knew it would require work on my part and, more importantly, prayer that God would not let that become a stronghold in my life. I began to wonder, *If this is the consequence of five seconds of pornographic material, what's the consequence of more of it?* In a nutshell, the consequence is destruction.

You may be confused about why I'm addressing pornography in a book intended primarily for young ladies. We tend to think of pornography as a "male problem." It is indeed a problem for many men, since one out of every two men admits to having a pornography addiction at some point in his life. They're not alone, though. Approximately one out of every five women admits to having a pornography addiction as well. That fact alone makes this a topic worth mentioning. What's more is the incredibly destructive power of pornography I alluded to earlier.

Here are three facts sexual purity ambassador, Laura Gallier, found during her research on pornography: First, just like hardcore drugs, pornography becomes addictive on a neurological level. In other words, pornography has the same effect on your brain as heroin or cocaine.

Next, pornography leads to increasingly worse depravity. For example, assume pornography has levels, ranging from 1 to 10. After you've watched Level 1 pornography for a while, it will not have the same effect on you. So you must move to Level 2. After a while, you will move to Level 3, then Level 4, and so on.

Lastly, pornography damages the reasoning center of the brain. Yes, watching pornography actually damages your ability to think rationally. Refer to Laura's blog on her website, lauragallier.com, to read the full article entitled *Pornography: There's no harm in looking, right?* You can also refer to that article to find help if you suffer from a pornography addiction.

Remember Ketchup

Our music, movie, and TV show selections can awaken, poke, and prod our sexual desires prematurely. Then, we either struggle to suppress them or we satisfy them outside of God's plan. This chapter is not a call to completely shut ourselves off from the world. Rather, it is a call to guard ourselves from those influences that will diminish our sexual purity. Sexually perverse music, movies, and TV shows are such influences.

Think back to our opening discussion about ketchup. Now think about what you're filling your mind with. If you and I say we want to resist sexual impurity, yet our choice of music, movies, and TV shows encourage it, we're lying to ourselves. If we're going to fight and win the battles in our minds, we must say *NO TRESPASSING* to all of that.

So, my friend, let's refuse to fill ourselves with material that will sabotage our mental victories over sexual impurity. Let's find healthy but quality alternatives in our music, movie, and television selections. Let's fill ourselves with whatever is true, noble, right, pure, lovely, admirable, excellent, or praiseworthy (Philippians 4:8). If we fill ourselves with these things, can you imagine what we'll see when this world *squeezes* us? We'll see righteousness, we'll see holiness, and we'll see sexually pure lives.

What's Next?

We've established that our journey of sexual purity begins in our minds. We know that our minds are naturally sinful, which means we have mental battles that we must fight and win. We've also identified a few pitfalls that prevent our mental victories over sexual impurity, such as our society's music, movies, and TV shows. So here's the next question: If our minds are naturally sinful, and our society has so much sexual impurity, how in the world can we be consistently victorious over sexual impurity? I'm so glad you asked! Continue with me to the next chapter to answer that question.

Reflection Questions:

Examine your iTunes library and your movie and TV show selections. What are you filling yourself with?

What comes out when you are squeezed (tempted)?

If your music, movie, and TV show selections are hurting your purity, what can you do over the next few weeks to make the necessary changes? What can you do today?

Prayer Starter:

Dear God,

Thank You for helping me see how important it is to guard my ears and my eyes. Please help me guard them against the sexual impurity that tries to poison them. Give me Your wisdom to perceive dangers and Your strength to stand firm. Fill me with Your holiness, so that's what comes out when this world squeezes me. In Jesus' name, Amen.

Chapter Three

MIND MAKEOVER

Out with the old, in with the new!

*"Do not conform any longer to the pattern of this world,
but be transformed by the renewing of your mind."*
Romans 12:2a

You Go, Girl

"Y ou look like a whole new person! You go, girl!" That's what everyone says after a lady gets a makeover on one of those talk shows. Don't you just love makeovers? I must admit, I love them too. Some of them can be quite amazing. No offense, but some of those ladies look pitiful at the beginning. Yet, after cutting a few things here, losing a few things there, replacing this and adding that, the result really does look like a whole new person.

You know what? That's exactly what our minds need—makeovers. You and I know that our minds can look really bad. For us to be consistently victorious over sexual impurity, our minds need to be made over. There must be some *cutting, losing, replacing,* and *adding* in our minds. Once that happens, our minds will begin to look brand new, just like a lady who has received a good makeover.

Cutting and Losing

What needs to be cut and lost from our minds? All the sinful, perverted, lustful, and overall ungodly thoughts and images in our minds. How do we cut and lose those thoughts and images? Well, I like to refer to a cool guy named Paul, who happens to be one of my favorite authors in the Bible. In 2 Corinthians 10:5, Paul writes, "…we take captive every thought to make it obedient to Christ."

As I've shared with you, I have not always abided by Paul's advice in this verse. There were times when I did not take any thoughts captive. I let them run around freely, and I even intentionally freed them at times. It wasn't until I started consistently capturing those thoughts and beating them into submission to Christ that I saw my mind truly begin to change.

By "take captive" Paul means you must stop the impure thoughts dead in their tracks. When that fantasy about a cute guy in your class or on your job begins to play, you click STOP immediately. Then, you "make it obedient to Christ" by, quite frankly, kicking it out of your mind. In other words, after you STOP the thought, you quickly DELETE it. That's how we cut and lose the bad stuff in our minds.

I'm not suggesting this process is as easy as stopping and deleting videos. To the contrary, it can be difficult and sometimes tiresome. However, its benefits far outweigh its costs. So we must do it. Sometimes, when I realize an inappropriate thought has crept into my mind, I will literally shake my head, as though I expect the thought to fly out of my ears. "Get out of there!" I demand. I don't recommend that you shake your head too hard or talk to yourself too loudly, especially when in the company of a lot of people. But hey, whatever works for you! You should cut and lose the sexual impurity in your mind, by any means necessary.

Replacing and Adding

Let's not forget the other part of making over our minds—replacing and adding. We've been taking out the old, perverse stuff, and now we must bring in the new, pure stuff. One of the best, most effective ways to suppress negative thoughts in our minds is to replace them with positive ones.

By what criteria can we decide if a thought is suitable to replace and add in our minds? I personally like the P48 criteria—that is, those given in Philippians 4:8. It says, "…whatever is true, whatever is noble, whatever is right, whatever is pure, whatever is lovely, whatever is admirable—if anything is excellent or praiseworthy—think about such things." What a list! Essentially, we can replace trashy thoughts with true ones, nasty thoughts with noble ones, perverse thoughts with pure ones, and so on.

Now, you may be thinking, *That sounds great and all, Leah, but it won't be easy. The bad thoughts are much easier to come by than the good ones.* Well, that may be true, and that's why I've found it helpful to have some safe, go-to thoughts "on file" in my mind.

For example, I love public speaking, and therefore I practically always have a speech rolling around in my head. So, when I'm seeking to release a negative thought, I will often grab a thought of me speaking. I'll envision myself giving a stirring speech to a massive, mesmerized crowd. I'll also envision the cute outfit and shoes I'm wearing, of course. Before I even finished writing this book, I would picture myself giving interviews about it at various churches and on radio shows.

These types of thoughts make up my mind's safe, go-to thoughts. I can quickly insert them in my mind after I've ejected bad thoughts. What could your safe, go-to thoughts be? If you're a dancer, could you envision yourself dancing before an adoring audience? If you're a singer, could you see yourself singing with your favorite recording artist? If you're an athlete, could you imagine yourself playing amazingly well in a playoff game? Whatever wholesome activity you love to do, I suggest you store up some thoughts about it from which you can pull later.

Cleaning House

I have an awesome mother. One of her many admirable qualities is her cleanliness. She just cannot *stand* a dirty house! It is for this reason she frequently cleans, straightens up, and throws away items in our home. Another quality of my mother's is that she likes to shop. So, every time she takes out an old item, she usually brings in a new one. This routine displays the old phrase, "Out with the old and in with the new." That saying and my mother's actions provide a great snapshot of how we make over our minds. Essentially, we must frequently throw out the old, perverted stuff in our minds (cut and lose) and bring in the new, pure stuff (replace and add).

Don't Try This Alone

Are you a strong-willed person? I am a *very* strong-willed person. When I get my mind set on something, that's it. (My mom calls it "stubbornness," but I prefer "strong will.") At one point, I began to feel guilty about eating so much fast food. That very day, I stopped eating burgers and fries. After a year or so, I released myself from the fast food ban, but I still won't allow myself to go *overboard* with fatty foods. Yeah, my will is made of bona fide steel.

Yet, when it comes to overcoming sexual lust, my willpower looks more like paper than steel. Don't get me wrong, our willpower can get us started on conquering sinful habits, and if we're exceptionally strong-willed, it can even carry us a few steps. But I must inform you that willpower is a flight risk. In the middle of fierce battles with temptation, our strong wills often crumble. Then, we end up back where we started, if not worse.

No, my friend, we cannot take on our "naughty natures" alone. Even Paul, one of Jesus' greatest apostles, said that when he wanted to do right, evil was always present (Romans 7:21). He goes on to talk about those two natures we Christians have within us—Spiritual and sinful. It is due to our dual natures that we can't rely on our own strength to make over our minds. You and I can't do this alone. We *must* rely on God's strength.

Only He holds the power to carry and sustain us on this sexual purity journey. This fact does not excuse us from taking practical steps to stay in line, like avoiding the trashy music, movies, and shows we discussed earlier. However, our reliance on God does give us confidence that we can make over our minds despite our weaknesses.

Give It To God

Essentially, God must be in charge of our mental makeovers, and we must rely on His expertise. What does this look like practically? How do we rely on the Lord for our mental makeovers? We do it the same way we plug into God's power, as we discussed in the "Battle Between the Ears" chapter. Let's dig a little deeper this time.

Psalm 119:9 asks and answers this question: How can a young person stay pure? The answer is by obeying God's Word. In order for God to make over our minds, we must study His Word. Reading and applying the Bible will grant us success in our sexual purity journeys and in our whole lives (Joshua 1:8). After reading a book, don't you know something about how its author thinks? Of course. Well, every word in the Bible has been inspired by God Himself (2 Timothy 3:16). Many people contributed to it, but He is the author. By studying the Bible, we learn to think more like God thinks, and that's basically how we allow Him to make over our minds.

I have another *very* important question: Do you like your hair to look nice? I sure do! I don't know about you, but if I don't believe someone knows what to do, I will not allow that person to style my hair. *Thanks, but no thanks.* Yet, when I believe someone does know what to do, my reaction drastically changes. I get snug in that seat, recline my head, and simply let the stylist do his or her thing.

Studying the Bible allows us to see that God always knows what to do. We learn that God can do anything, even make over our minds. These realizations help us trust Him more. When we begin to see just how abundantly qualified God is, we will respond to Him the same way we respond to qualified hair stylists—we'll relax and just let Him do His thing.

Prayer is another way we rely on God's strength for our mental makeovers. Is it fair to expect someone to meet our needs, if we never express our needs to him or her? Not really. In any relationship, communication is important. The same is true of our relationship with God. It's true that unlike people, God already knows what we need. Even so, frequently communicating with Him displays our reliance on Him.

It's mainly for our own benefit that we should talk to God about our needs. We can often find encouragement and power when we do so. When we pray, we should be open and honest with the Lord about our struggles and thank Him in advance for helping us overcome them.

Studying the Bible and praying are great. However, they won't do us much good if we don't apply what we learn to our daily lives. Good thing God has given us a Helper to assist us in doing just that (John 14:26). The world calls it a conscience, but we should call it the Holy Spirit.

Obeying the Holy Spirit is the final way we rely on the Lord for our mental makeovers. The Holy Spirit is God living in us, and He will show us practical ways to make over our minds. So when we close our Bibles, finish our prayer times, and go about our daily routines, we must still follow God's lead through the Holy Spirit. When we do, we will begin to see miraculous changes in our own minds.

We Will Never "Arrive"

You should not expect to "arrive" at a perfectly made-over mind. I know, you're probably thinking, *Leah, are you kidding me? Did you really just give me all these pointers about making over my mind, only to tell me I'll never arrive?* Calm down, my friend. I simply mean we should be careful not to get too comfortable or become *sexual purity snobs*.

When I share my testimony about being a virgin and guarding my purity, I do not do so in a spirit of pride. Throughout my life, the Lord has shielded and blocked for me in this area of sexual purity. I am what I am only by the grace of God (1 Corinthians 15:10). My testimony is a gift from God, and I share it as such. I never want to reach a place where I *think* I've got it all together. The Bible warns us that "Pride goes before destruction, a haughty spirit before a fall" (Proverbs 16:18). Basically, this verse says that along the "I can do no wrong" road is a deep pit called destruction. If we make a habit of traveling down that prideful road, we're liable to find ourselves at the bottom of that pit.

If we lived sexually pure yesterday, that doesn't give us a right to be prideful today. Yes, we can reap the benefits of yesterday's good choices, but we cannot rest on them. No matter where we think we fall on the sexual purity spectrum, we all have something in common: We must continually make over our minds—day by day, hour by hour, minute by minute, moment by moment.

Mind Makeover = Life Makeover

As you make over your mind, you will be amazed by the changes you'll see in your life. Since there's very little we can control in this world, changing the way we think is the most effective way to change our lives. This truth applies to our sexual purity journeys too. The mind makeover is a necessity for this journey. Why? Because it's the made-over mind that will keep us moving in the right direction.

As with athletics, our sexual purity has a powerful mental component. Plenty of athletes possess the physical toughness to accomplish tasks, but they lack the mental toughness to do so. If someone has the physical durability to run a 1,500m race but doesn't have the proper attitude to endure, will she be successful? Nope; she *could* do it, but she won't. If someone has the physical strength to lift 500 pounds but has a weak mind, do you think she'll be successful? Not likely; she *could* do it, but she won't. Likewise, we all *can* live sexually pure lives, but if we don't partner with the Lord to make over our minds, we won't. So I'm scheduling a makeover for my mind today and every day for the rest of my life. How about you?

Reflection Questions:

What are some new, pure thoughts that can replace your old, impure ones?

Have you been depending on the Lord's strength to renew your mind or your own? How can you make sure you depend on the Lord's strength?

Prayer Starter:

Dear God,

Please transform my mind today, tomorrow, and every day for the rest of my life. Help me uproot the perversion in my mind, and help me plant thoughts that please You. I don't want to be a slave to my sinful mind. Please make over my mind. Please make over my life. In Jesus' name, Amen.

Section Two

Chapter Four

VICTORIA NOT-SO-SECRET

What messages do your clothes send?

"I also want the women to dress modestly, with decency and propriety."
1 Timothy 2:9a

What's Your Message?

Sometimes, the way we dress sends a message. Let me rephrase that: *All the time*, the way we dress sends a message. Some messages are ones of purity. This occurs when we wear flattering but not overly exposing clothes. Conversely, other outfits send messages of impurity. This happens when we wear excessively tight, short, or revealing clothes. Wearing such clothing causes us to give off sexual signals. Whether we acknowledge it or not, those clothes act as an invitation for others to view our bodies as sex objects.

Are You a Treasure or a Target?

My dad likes to watch nature shows, and he really likes the ones that highlight predators and their prey. As I've walked in and out of his *man cave* (our game room) over the years, I've heard about many different predator-prey interactions. There's one thing I've never heard, though. I've never heard of any prey trying to get its predator's attention. In fact, the predator's attention is usually the last thing the prey desires. Can you imagine a squirrel actually *trying* to get a hawk's attention?

In our world, some guys are predators. When we dress immodestly, we are more likely to get their attention. These guys may not necessarily want to injure us, but they do want to rob us of our virtue and our conviction to stay pure. My friend shared a great question with me from Chad Eastman: Are we dressing like treasures or targets? Ultimately, those are the only two options. Either we dress like the treasures God created us to be, or we dress like targets for predators to chase. Dressing like targets would be like a squirrel trying to get a hawk's attention—unwise.

I do not believe dressing immodestly justifies guys viewing us as targets or sex objects. And I strongly reject the idea that dressing immodestly gives anyone the right to disrespect or violate us. Sexual assault is *never* acceptable. What I do believe is that dressing immodestly sends messages of sexual impurity, and that sending such messages has negative consequences.

Stop Trying to be Like "Them"

This concept of dressing modestly may be especially difficult for us to grasp, because everywhere we look in our society, we see *sexy* women. We constantly see women who wear super tight, super short, super revealing clothes. Most of the top musical artists, fashion models, and actresses dress this way, and it seems as though everyone glorifies them. Our culture considers these women to be the perfect examples of beauty and sexuality. It's no wonder many of us try to look like them.

One day I expressed my frustration to my god-sister, Jennifer. I admitted to her that when I saw the "popular girls" at my university, I sometimes felt tinges of sadness, jealously, and inferiority. I told her that I would often wonder, *What do they have that I don't have?* Then I would think, *Well for starters, Leah, you don't have those super short shorts, those super high heels, or that super low top!* My god-sister chuckled and then replied, "Leah, keep in mind that you can always be one of those ladies, but those ladies cannot be you."

What Jennifer meant by that statement is this: At any moment, I could begin to wear more exposing clothes, attract more guys, give those guys my virginity and virtue, and consequently be like those young ladies. However, those young ladies could not as easily be like me— someone who had not dressed provocatively or given away her virginity and virtue. She encouraged me to remain true to myself and to view my worth with the proper perspective.

I want to make something very clear. When my god-sister said those young ladies could not be me, she did not mean they could *never* become virtuous, pure ladies. Even the most immodest and most immoral women can ask God for forgiveness and commit their lives to Him. If they do, He will forgive them, restore their virtue, and redeem them.

Have you ever known someone who always brings up your past mistakes? Well, God is *not* like that. When we sincerely ask God to forgive us for our mistakes, He completely removes those mistakes from us. Psalm 103:12 says, "As far as the east is from the west, so far has he removed our transgressions from us."

Even if you've slept with many different guys, when God forgives you, you can become what some call a *born-again virgin.* That means, in the eyes of God, you will no longer be defined by that promiscuous past.

He can and will use you for His glory. In fact, some of the great women of God in the Bible had immoral pasts; some were former prostitutes and former adulterers. I don't know your past, but please don't ever believe the lie that you are too far gone.

That being said, I must note that we can never get back our physical virginity. That's a gift we can give away only once. The Lord did some great things through formerly promiscuous women, but He did great things through women of virtue, too. After all, He chose a young virgin named Mary to be the mother of Jesus. If you still have your physical virginity, cherish and protect it. If you don't, be encouraged that you can receive that *born-again virginity* in God's eyes.

So when we see those barely dressed, overly sexual women on the reality T.V. shows, commercials, music videos, and magazines, let's not desire to be like them. Instead, let's remember this: As virtuous ladies of God, we can easily become like those women at any moment, but they cannot easily become like us.

How we present ourselves sends a message, and we should be sure it's a message of purity. That means we must frequently check the messages of what we wear. How do we do that? We examine our motives. While we try on clothes, we should ask ourselves, *What are my motives for choosing this particular top or bottom or dress? What responses do I expect or desire from others?* If showing off our bodies or drawing attention to ourselves motivates us to choose an outfit, that outfit will not send a good message.

Don't forget that we can cover up and still look cute. I call it the *C&C look*—Covered and Cute! In that case, it's perfectly fine if people notice us or compliment our outfits. Getting attention and compliments simply should not be our *motivation* for deciding what to wear. We cannot control how people receive our messages, but we can control what messages we send. So before we step outside, let's check our messages.

The Guy Factor

Our culture's "popular ladies" play a role in our struggles to dress modestly, but I think another group of people play a bigger role—the guys. Let's be honest, my friend. Can you honestly say you don't like getting positive attention from guys? Especially from the cute ones? Most of us like it. Often times, ladies wear clothes they believe will catch guys' attention. This practice represents the influence of "the guy factor." I have struggled with "the guy factor." I had to confront it after an experience I had in college.

One day, I woke up later than I intended. I didn't want to be late for class, so I rolled out of bed, washed my face, threw on the first top and jeans I saw, and ran out the door. I had walked a considerable distance from my dorm, when all of the sudden, I felt a breeze on my chest. I looked down and quickly discovered that my top had obviously shrunken in the dryer. I now had cleavage showing that I didn't have before!

I was too far away and too late to go back and change, so I kept walking. I didn't think it was a big deal, until I encountered some guys. Oh. My. Goodness. They smiled and winked and waved at me. Apparently, these guys approved of my top's lower-cut neckline. A part of me really liked this extra attention, and I wondered, *Hmm, if I keep wearing cleavage-bearing tops, will I keep getting extra attention from guys?*

I knew the answer was probably "yes," but thankfully, I decided not to dress like that again. As nice as I thought those double-takes and smiles were, I knew they were shallow. Any guy who would approach me for my cleavage would not be interested in Whose I am or who I am. That guy would also not be with me for long, seeing as there are many cleavage-bearing ladies around the world. I reminded myself (and still do remind myself) that the Lord has called me to be set apart, so I need not walk around looking like everyone else. He has called you and me to use our bodies to honor Him, not to attract people to ourselves (1 Corinthians 6:19-20).

Since I decided not to let "the guy factor" guide my clothing choices, does that mean I do not like attention from guys? Absolutely not! I do indeed like it. Most of us appreciate affirmation of our attractiveness from anybody, but especially from members of the opposite sex. I believe it's okay and even natural to appreciate guys' attention and flattery.

What's not okay is to dress immodestly due to an excessive longing for their attention and compliments. We should not depend on the flattery of guys, and we certainly should not base our self-worth on it. We must check and often change the value we place on males' attention. Is this easy? No. Is it necessary for our sexual purity, though? Absolutely.

If we depend on the approval of guys, we will be more likely to give away our virtue in the hopes of feeling valued and loved by them. This dependence will also cause us to live restless, unfulfilled lives. Even if we receive 100,000 compliments, we will long for compliment number 100,001. No matter how many men praise us, their approval will never make us feel complete. Only God can do that.

In general, we can never win the people-pleasing game, and we who believe in Christ Jesus should not even play that game. Our top priority should be to please God in all aspects of our lives, including the way we dress. Galatians 1:10 reads, "Am I now trying to win the approval of men, or of God? Or am I trying to please men? If I were still trying to please men, I would not be a servant of Christ."

Need I say more? That verse is abundantly clear. An obsession with pleasing people cripples our service to Christ. So, as difficult as it may be at times, let's release ourselves from the burden of pleasing others. When we pick out our clothes, let's forget "the guy factor" and remember "the God factor." Let's seek to please God alone. When we do so, we will be free, and we will be the Father's *fashionistas!*

What's All That *Really* Worth?

I continually pray that God will help me get and keep a proper perspective on others' opinions of me. I take this seriously, because as we discussed, an unbalanced value on guys' attention can negatively impact our modesty. What's more, this same unbalanced value on males' attention can cause us to compromise our sexual purity.

Our culture has conditioned us to believe that guys' desires for us validate our femininity and our beauty. We've been groomed to think that guys' sexual advances affirm our worth and equate love. They call out to us, they whistle, they honk their car horns, and they flirt, leading us to believe those actions are of great worth.

But how much is all that *really* worth? When guys approach us in those ways, are they really interested in us? Do they care anything about who we are, Whose we are, our fears and failures, our hopes and dreams? Most likely not. Those approaches usually mean those guys are interested in our looks. Our physical appearance is an aspect of who we are, but it is not the only aspect; and it is certainly not the most important one. If guys approach us based solely on their physical attraction to us, what happens when they come across someone else they find attractive? If our immodest attire and behavior attracts them, how will they respond to the next woman's immodest attire and behavior? At the end of the day, those guys are truly saying, "I'll give you my momentary attention in exchange for your virtue." And in reality, guys' momentary attention does not amount to much. So giving up our virtue for it would not be a fair exchange.

To see this point more clearly, consider my experience at a local smoothie place. I ordered a small strawberry-banana smoothie (my personal favorite). The cashier told me my total was $3.50. As I reached for my money, the cashier gave me a proposition: I could have the smoothie for free in exchange for my name and number. *Hmm...* I really like to save my money, so I considered this proposal!

I first began to think about my name. My parents actually put thought into my first name, Leah. There's a woman named Leah in the Bible. Each time she cried out to the Lord, He heard her cry and blessed her. My father prayed the Lord would always hear my cries to Him and bless me too. My maiden name, Holder, gives me a sense of belonging to my father and his lineage. It gives me assurance that he is my dad, and I am his daughter. Moreover, my full name is more than just a name, because it carries my reputation along with it. All things considered, I concluded that my name has great value to me.

Then, I thought about my phone number. When I give people my phone number, it gives them unlimited access to me. They can text or call me at any time. That doesn't mean I will respond or pick up at any time, but they can do it nevertheless. Aside from business reasons, there is a certain level of closeness involved with giving someone my number. So it has value to me as well.

When I finished thinking about all these things, I concluded giving that guy my name and number in exchange for a $3.50 smoothie simply wasn't a fair exchange. Giving him things of such great value in exchange for something so cheap and unfulfilling just didn't make sense to me.

And you know what, my friend? I've concluded the same thing about my virginity, about my virtue. I refuse to give away something so valuable in exchange for things so cheap. I refuse to give away my virtue in exchange for $3.50 affection, $3.50 attention, $3.50 false declarations of love, $3.50 empty compliments, and the like. I constantly pray for the Lord to help me guard myself, so that I don't dress or behave in ways that will cost me my virginity or my virtue.

I pray the same for you, this entire generation of ladies, and those to come. I don't want to see any more young ladies, especially those within the body of Christ, give away things of such great value in exchange for things so cheap and unfulfilling. Proverbs 31:10 says, "Who can find a virtuous woman? For her price is far above rubies." Rubies are some of the most valuable jewels in the world, and God says virtuous women are worth *far more*. You wouldn't exchange rubies for $3.50, so please don't exchange your virtue for cheap fees either. We are of such great worth in the eyes of God, and our virtue is a precious gift. I desperately want all ladies to know that. I desperately want *you* to know that.

There is no fair exchange for our virtue or for our purity. And the *only* fair exchange for our virginity is a life-long marital covenant declared before God and a minister or judge. It would also be nice to have family and friends there to take pictures of us in our pretty wedding dresses!

Will You Be a Leaf or a Diamond?

I love my conversations with my Grandma Josie. One of the best pieces of advice I've received regarding modesty came from her. She said, "Leah, you young ladies just need to leave something to the imagination!" I laughed and shook my head. Yet, as I observed what many young ladies wear, I better understood my Grandma's words. I noticed that many ladies' clothing left nothing to people's imaginations. We don't have to imagine what we can clearly see.

Some ladies' clothes are so short, so fitted, and so exposing, that anyone who looks at them can easily perceive their entire bodies. At times, some of these ladies wonder why they do not get the respect they deserve. The answer is simple, though: Exclusive things are usually more respected than public things.

Consider leaves and diamonds. Which one do we value more in our society, the leaves or the diamonds? Due to their high value within our ecosystem, we *should* hold leaves in high regard. Yet, because we see them so often, we tend to disregard them, sweep them to the side, and even throw them away sometimes.

But what if we were to stumble upon an authentic diamond? We would not ignore it, and we certainly would not throw it away! On the contrary, we would take hold of it, cherish it, and view it with very high regard. Why? Because real diamonds are far less common than leaves. While we can come by leaves with great ease, it usually takes great effort or sacrifice to come by a real diamond. If diamonds grew on trees as leaves do, would we value them as highly? Probably not. We would grow accustomed to seeing them all the time and thus value them less.

Likewise, every woman's body *should* be held in high regard, because every woman is a creation of the Most High God. Every woman has great value. However, it will be difficult for others to respect ladies who expose their bodies. As many do to leaves, some guys will disregard these ladies' worth, sweep their dignity to the side, and even throw them away once they've used them. It's not right, but it's reality.

Human nature involves placing higher value on things that are less available. Essentially, that's why we undervalue leaves, and that's why guys undervalue immodest women. Diamonds and leaves do not get to choose what they will be, but we do. Every time we decide what to wear and how to behave, we get to choose. So I'm choosing to be a diamond. How about you?

Don't Forget the Good Guys

So who exactly receives the messages our clothes send? Everybody who sees us! Yes, even the good guys. Let's be mindful of our brothers in Christ and their pursuit of sexual purity. Guys who seriously pursue sexual purity don't want to see the sexually impure messages some of our outfits send. When looking for potential mates, these guys view such impure messages as turn-offs. Wouldn't it be a shame if our attempts to attract a good guy actually had the opposite effect and pushed good guys away?

At the same time, these good guys battle their "naughty natures" just as we do. Since guys tend to be more visually stimulated than ladies, our lack of modesty can pose big stumbling blocks to their progress. So, before we step outside, we should consider the few guys who do work to discipline their eyes and minds, and who truly seek to honor God. If we even slightly think our clothing may be a hindrance to their purity, we should reconsider wearing it.

Now, don't get too carried away with this idea. Don't constantly obsess over being a stumbling block to guys and end up wearing outfits that don't flatter your body or fit your age. Just use your common sense. God has created us beautifully, so some guys will be attracted to us even if we wear sweat pants and oversized t-shirts. We can't help that. But when it comes to making guys drool with skin-tight miniskirts and low-cut tops, we *can* help that. It can also be helpful to think about the following question: If you were to see your boyfriend, husband, or son talking to a lady dressed like you, would you feel comfortable or uneasy? If you'd feel uneasy, I think you know what that means.

Let's Do This Thing

I encourage you to champion modesty, my friend. I'm not saying we have to wear nothing but turtlenecks and skirts that drag on the floor as we walk. I am saying that we should continually examine our intentions behind what we wear. We should assess what messages our clothes send about us, and we should consider whether our clothing may be a hindrance to the sexual purity of others. If we truly desire a sexually pure lifestyle, our clothes should display that desire. Let's not only write, read, and talk about living modestly, but let's also do it. Let's tell immodesty there will be *NO TRESPASSING*.

Reflection Questions:

When you try on clothes, how do you decide what to wear and what not to wear? Do guys' reactions play a role in your decisions?

What type of guys do you attract most of the time? Does that answer tell you anything about the messages you're sending?

If you don't attract many guys, how does that make you feel about yourself? What does your answer to that question tell you about the importance you place on guys' opinions of you?

Do you believe your clothes send messages of sexual purity? If not, what can you do in the next few weeks to change your messages? What can you do today?

Prayer Starter:

Dear God,

I thank You that I am beautifully and wonderfully made. I'm so thankful that my worth's validation comes from You alone. I know You have called me to dress modestly. Please forgive me for all the times I have not lived up to Your high calling. Give me all I need to reject this world's dress code and embrace Yours. In Jesus' name, Amen.

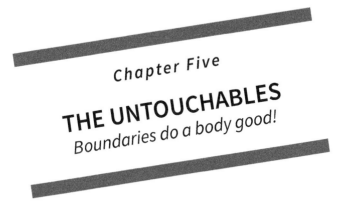

Chapter Five

THE UNTOUCHABLES

Boundaries do a body good!

"Do you not know that your bodies are temples of the Holy Spirit, who is in you, whom you have received from God? You are not your own; you were bought at a price. Therefore honor God with your bodies.
1 Corinthians 6:19-20

Beautiful Boundaries

What do many people put in place to keep outsiders from trespassing on their private property? A fence, a gate, or some sort of boundary, right? Well, in order to protect our bodies from trespassing, we must set up boundaries too. Our boundaries for our relationships with guys should be clear and well thought out. Consider a few examples of what clear physical boundaries may include: No being alone in each other's rooms or homes, no touching all over each other's bodies, giving each other only distant frontal hugs (leave some space between your lower bodies), no making out, and so on.

I am not saying these boundaries *must* be your boundaries; I'm simply providing examples of clear boundaries. Having such clear boundaries will ensure we know what is and isn't acceptable. If there's one thing we don't want in our relationships, it is confusion. And I must warn you that confusion and sin have a *very* good friendship. Boundaries help us avoid that confusion and stay in line. Conversely, without such boundaries, we're liable to wander into dangerous territory. Before we know it, we may allow people to trespass on our bodies, and we may simultaneously trespass on theirs.

Kissing Can Get You Pregnant

You may be thinking, *How could I unknowingly wander into a sexual danger zone? I'll see it coming, so I'll know when to stop!* Well, we must be careful, because physical contact usually progresses over time. Often times, physical contact begins with actions that seem perfectly innocent at first. I once heard an old lady say, "Kissing can get you pregnant!" I literally laughed out loud, shaking my head in disbelief. After I thought about it, though, I perceived some truth in her comment.

Obviously, kissing in and of itself cannot get anyone pregnant. However, kissing can cause progressively more intense physical contact. It does in fact arouse our bodies and prepare them for sexual intercourse. All of this can happen so quickly.

Many people start off just holding hands. Then they move to light touching, then they lightly kiss each other on the mouth, then the kissing and touching get more intense, and you see where I'm going. By no means do I suggest it happens *exactly* like this. I'm simply showing how *innocent* actions can progress into less innocent actions over time.

As my friend says, "The further we go, the further we want to go." So we must be careful.

No Take Backs

When should we set these clear boundaries? At the beginning of any relationship. Doing so is far, far better than trying to go back after the fact. Let's not wait until we're alone with someone on the couch and the situation starts getting heated. This situation would not be the most practical or most effective time to put boundaries in place. In fact, avoiding this scenario (being all alone with someone on the couch) should probably be a boundary in itself.

Moving in reverse with our physical interactions is not impossible, but it is very difficult. And once two people have had sex with one another, trying to *pump the brakes* becomes even more difficult. Often times, those couples have to separate in order to stop having sex. Some of them get back together, but others don't. This reality is why it's so important and helpful to put those boundaries in place at the beginning.

How Far is Too Far?

After I speak to groups of young ladies, some of the most frequent questions I receive are: When on a date, how far is too far? Can we do *this*? Should we do *that*? However, I've realized that those are not the best questions. The best question we can ask ourselves before we do anything is this: Will this action honor God? If the answer is "yes," go for it. If the answer is "no," don't do it. If we have to debate it in our minds for a while, the answer is probably "no."

As we briefly discussed in the Introduction, the primary reason Christians should live sexually pure is to honor God, our Father. When we honor Him with pure lives, we unlock the door to greater intimacy (or closeness) with Him. Many women spend their whole lives looking for true intimacy in sex and relationships with guys, but true intimacy can be found only in God. And please believe me, my friend, there are no words to describe the beauty of drawing closer to God!

If we do not live pure, He will still love us, but there will be a noticeable disconnection in our fellowship with Him. I once heard Priscilla Shirer share a story that perfectly illustrates this truth. She said that she and her husband were on a flight with their infant son. Her husband was holding their son close to his chest, rubbing his little back and kissing his little face. Priscilla smiled and drifted asleep. A little while later, she was awakened by a smell. She soon discovered that the source of the smell was none other than her baby boy. She opened her eyes and found that her husband was no longer cuddling with their baby but was now holding him out at a distance!

In that moment, Priscilla's husband was still their baby's father, and he did still love his son. He just couldn't be in close fellowship with his son due to the smelly *mess* the son was in. Likewise, when we Christians have patterns of sin in our lives, especially sexual sin, we disrupt our close fellowship with God. In those moments, He is still our Father, and He does still love us. He just can't be in close fellowship with us when we're in smelly *messes*. Why? Because He is holy (Psalm 99:9).

So if we determine that an action will not honor God, but we feel as though we want to do it anyway, perhaps the next question we should ask is this: Is the temporary pleasure I'll get from this action worth fracturing my fellowship with my Father? I pray you will decide, as I have, that the answer is always "no." Absolutely nothing is worth compromising our communion with our Father. Knowing that truth is not enough, though. We must have boundaries.

Run, Girl, Run

So how can we know what our personal boundaries should look like? Well, boundaries will vary from person to person, but we must be honest with ourselves. Some of us may be able to handle more than others, but we all have limits. We should know our limits and refuse to push them. The Bible tells us to *flee* from sexual immorality (1 Corinthians 6:18). It does not say to *flirt* with it.

If you were on a cliff, would you try to see how close you could get to the edge of that cliff without falling off? I sure wouldn't. It seems to me that the only way you could truly find that answer, would be to reach the point where you actually fall off the cliff. Then, as you're falling, you could say, "That second to last step was the closest I could get to the edge without falling off!" How else could you know for sure which point was the point of no return?

Perhaps you're simply a more courageous "nature lady" than I am, and I don't fault you for that. But when it comes to our sexual purity boundaries, the objective is *not* to see how close we can get to the edge without falling off. Rather, we should strive to keep as much distance between us and the edge as possible! If we don't, we may reach that point of no return and then have to bear the painful consequences of falling into sexual sin.

With each inappropriate sexual action, we move closer to the edge; we lose portions of our virtue. *Every* action counts. There is no middle ground. As with the cliff illustration, the only way we could know for sure where our point of no return is, would be to reach that point and *not* return. Personally, I don't want to know where my breaking point is, because if I find out, that means it's too late—that means I've fallen.

I encourage you, my friend, not to flirt with the edge but to flee from it. We don't need to know how close we can get without falling. All we need to know is that if we put godly boundaries in place, we can guard ourselves from falling.

So let's be honest with ourselves when we set up our boundaries. If you can handle holding hands, then good for you. But if you can't handle it, don't do it. If you can handle light kissing, then hats off to you. But if you can't handle it, don't do it. I'm not sure anyone can engage in heavy kissing and touching without becoming sexually aroused, so I think it's safe to say *all* of us should avoid those actions. We must be honest with ourselves, so we can put ourselves in positions to succeed. I want to set myself up to win! Don't you?

Learning Curve

Will we get these boundaries right all the time? Nope. We do have to learn some things as we go. One morning when I was in high school, a football player gave me a close, firm, frontal hug. And it was that very morning I learned to *avoid* close, firm, frontal hugs! I am now a big fan of the *side* hug. Some time later, a guy I dated found out how ticklish I am. He began to tickle me more and more frequently and aggressively. I could foresee that getting out of control one day, so I established a no-more-tickling policy.

Some people may think those boundaries seem extreme, but as I've stated before, we must do what's necessary to stay on track. I know of a couple who did not hold hands until they were engaged and did not kiss until their wedding day. I'm sure people told them that their boundaries were "extreme." Yet, they both entered their marriage sexually pure, and now they enjoy a happy, healthy marriage. That's much more than I can say for many other married couples in our society. So, if some "extreme" pre-marriage boundaries are the price we must pay for healthy marriages, let's pay it! Couples with no boundaries end up paying a far greater price.

Safe Way

My father, who I affectionately call Daddy "O," has several phrases he repeats *all* the time. I like to call them *Daddy "O"isms*. One of his notorious *Daddy "O"isms* is "Err on the side of caution." What my dad means by that statement is this: It's better to be too careful than not careful enough.

For example, I'm not sure if I could handle making out or not. Since there's only one way to find out, I've just decided not to do it. I'd rather be too careful and say, "I'm in control of myself," than not be careful enough and say, "Oops…" Experience can be a good teacher at times, but I prefer Wisdom as my teacher. To the best of our ability, we should limit the learn-as-we-go lessons. When it comes to our boundaries, let's just play it safe!

I strongly recommend you develop a purity plan, because it will help you create your boundaries. Think about questions such as the following: When do you struggle the most to stay sexually pure? What leads up to those tempting situations? Where are you? Who are you with? What are you doing? Use your answers to those questions and the Reflection Questions to start developing your purity plan and boundaries. We are much more likely to actually do things after we write them down, so feel free to use the space on the next page and the Notes pages in the back of the book.

Reflection Questions:

Have you been fleeing from sexual impurity or flirting with it? Can you think of a recent example?

If you've been flirting with sexual impurity, what changes can you make to begin fleeing it?

What physical boundaries do you need to put in place for your relationships?

Are your boundaries clear? Have you been honest with yourself about your limitations? Explain.

Prayer Starter:

Dear God,

Thank You for calling me to be holy, to be set apart, to be untouchable to impurity. Please give me the wisdom, the strength, and the resolve to put physical boundaries in place for my relationships. I know You desire to protect me, and I know I have a part to play in my protection too. Enable me to play my part and play it well. In Jesus' name, Amen.

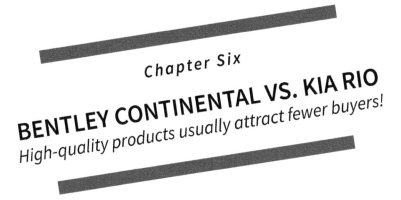

Chapter Six

BENTLEY CONTINENTAL VS. KIA RIO
High-quality products usually attract fewer buyers!

"If the world hates you, keep in mind that it hated me first."
John 15:18

Life of Luxury

Dressing modestly and putting boundaries in place may not go over so well with some guys. We may begin to feel as though we're at a disadvantage to women who have no standards. In this "competitive market" of guys, it may seem as though those women are attracting all the potential buyers. We see a similar phenomenon in the car industry, don't we? Consider the Bentley Continental and the Kia Rio. At this time, the Bentley Continental Supersports will cost you around $320,000! The Kia Rio, on the other hand, will cost you around $14,000. (Just for the record, I have nothing against Kia Rios!)

Let's imagine the Bentley and the Kia car lots sit side-by-side. Which one do you think will have more potential buyers walking around it? Typically, the lots selling cheaper cars have more people on them than those of luxury cars. Even though a lot of people may desire luxury cars, not many people can afford them. However, of the few who do go to the luxury car lots, many of them can actually afford to purchase cars of such high quality.

What does all of this have to do with us and our standards? Well, for our purposes, *potential buyers* represent guys who pursue us and *to purchase* means to make a true commitment. Now, please do not take this analogy literally. We have *immensely* more worth than cars, and we certainly should not be purchased under any circumstances. Moreover, even the most immoral women are not cheap in the eyes of God. But in the eyes of men, these ladies are viewed a certain way, namely as sex objects. So ladies with low or no standards do tend to attract more guys. When we raise the standards of how we dress, and when we set up boundaries with guys, we become like Bentley Continentals—we become luxury ladies!

As luxury ladies, we may not attract as many guys as non-luxury ladies do. And when we do attract guys, some of them may become less interested once they discover our luxury lady status. These guys have not prepared to purchase (or make a true commitment to) a lady of such high quality.

I've experienced this scenario a few times. In high school, a certain guy flirted with me every day. He would carry my books and walk me to class. But once he discovered my standards, things changed. Let's just say I had to start carrying my own books to class! Since then, there have been other guys who liked me but just weren't willing to abide by my values.

Yeah, it disappoints me a bit, but God always helps me get over it relatively quickly. He reminds me that even though many guys have not prepared themselves for luxury ladies, some guys have. Just as some buyers will be prepared to purchase luxury cars when they approach those car lots, some guys will be prepared to make true commitments to luxury ladies when they approach us. So let's value the quality of our suitors over the quantity of them. Speaking of quality guys, continue with me to the next section.

He's No King

Some guys do intentionally look for women lacking both modesty and physical boundaries, but what do you think these men value? Do they care for these women? No, as we discussed in the "Victoria Not-So-Secret" chapter, these guys value the superficial aspects of women, and they tend to be uninterested in making true commitments. I once heard a preacher say that there are guys who seek women without modesty and boundaries, but that they are not kings. Therefore, if we enter into relationships with them, we should not expect to be treated like queens. What a great point!

So perhaps we should stop craving the attention of mere *commoners*. These are guys with no interest in God or His purpose for our lives. Instead, we should constantly pursue God's will and prepare for our kings to find us.

I should note that this is not an exact science. Every guy interested in a modest woman is not necessarily a "good guy," and every man interested in an immodest woman is not necessarily a "bad guy." For instance, even though I do dress modestly and have boundaries, I have attracted some not-so-good guys in passing. However, of those who have pursued a serious relationship with me, they have been mostly good guys.

I also cannot prove the claim that every guy interested in immodest women is a bad guy. Yet, I believe most people will agree that guys who approach half-dressed, no-boundaries ladies have more interest in those ladies' bodies than anything else about them. By dressing modestly and guarding our bodies, we can weed out most commoners and therefore more easily spot the kings. It's possible we may attract fewer suitors, but there's a greater chance God's mate for us is among those we do attract.

Takes One to Know One

Since we're on the topic of assessing guys who pursue us, I'd like to address a few quotes from the CEO of Building Lasting Relationships, Dr. Clarence Shuler. First, he says, "Instead of worrying about finding the right person, singles should focus on *being* the right person, because God won't bring his best to a mess." I love that quote! Essentially, Dr. Shuler suggests that instead of frantically looking for our kings, we should work on becoming queens. If we do so, we will be prepared when God brings our kings.

How do we work on becoming queens? Well, we've already discussed that we should dress and behave as queens or *luxury ladies*. Another helpful tip I've learned is this: Make sure you meet the criteria you hope for in a mate. For instance, I pray and hope for a mate who loves and fears God, consistently exercises self-discipline, has an easy-going personality, and lives sexually pure. So, I must examine my own life and see if I meet those criteria.

Do I love and fear God? Do I consistently exercise self-discipline? Do I have an easy-going personality? Do I live sexually pure? If I cannot consistently answer "yes" to these questions, that means I have work to do. Do you possess the characteristics you hope for in a mate? As Dr. Shuler suggests, while we wait on God's best, we should work on cleaning up our mess.

My Grandma Josie echoed Dr. Shuler's point and added one of her own in a conversation I had with her.

Me: Yeah, Grandma, I don't want to just marry someone. I want to marry the *right* someone.

Grandma: I understand, baby.

Me: I think just about anyone can marry, but I want to marry well... and stay married!

Grandma: I know what you mean!

Me: But the Lord has shown me that I must learn to be satisfied in my current season of life. I can't wait until I get married to start enjoying my life. I think some single ladies believe marriage will solve all their problems, but that's not true.

Grandma: No, that's not true. And if those single ladies have a lot of problems, they probably should stay single!

Me: [Laughing out loud]

Grandma: Only God can fix our lives, baby.

Me: Yes ma'am, Grandma. Yes ma'am.

My Grandma possesses great wisdom! In essence, she agrees with Dr. Shuler's assertion that we should work on our "mess" if we want God's best. She also adds this truth: Only God can truly clean up our mess. We can take practical steps to help, such as study the Bible, pray, obey the Holy Spirit, dress modestly, behave decently, and so on. Yet, at the end of the day, only God can clean up our lives.

Our lives will never be spotless, because we are fallible humans living in an imperfect world. However, the more we allow God to work certain traits in us and other ones out of us, the better prepared we will be for our future mates.

The Good or The Best

I'm equally enthused about Dr. Shuler's next quote: "One of the enemy's greatest tactics is convincing us to settle for good instead of God's best." I pondered this second quote for a while, especially in regards to evaluating potential mates. The enemy knows most of us will not fall for obviously awful guys. Several ladies admit to finding bad boys attractive, but I don't know of too many ladies who desire to actually marry one. Most of us aren't tempted to settle that lowly. Rather, we are more likely tempted to settle for a good guy instead of waiting on God's best guy for us.

Plenty of guys appear to be good guys, but we must resolve to look beyond the surface. For example, should the facts that certain guys go to church, publicly treat us with respect, and abide by the law, automatically qualify them as our mates? Don't get me wrong, those are all great, upstanding qualities. However, to me, such qualities are the equivalent of putting your name on an application. Without your name on it, your application won't even be considered by an employer. Likewise, we should not even consider marrying guys without those qualities. Their applications should be denied automatically!

Those qualities are *required* for potential mates, but they do not *guarantee* that someone is God's mate for you or me. We must consider many other factors and components of their character, and, as I mentioned, we should look beyond the surface. Yes, the guy goes to church, but does he truly have a personal relationship with Jesus Christ? Yes, he treats you well in public (he opens doors, pays for meals, etc.), but how does he treat you in private? Also, most guys will treat us well when they're trying to win us over, but how do they treat their parents and their long-time friends? Yes, the guy abides by the law, but shouldn't he do that anyway? These are just a few questions to consider before making judgments about a guy's character. Let's be careful about giving credit where it isn't due.

Please don't take my observations as a call for us to be super picky and overly critical of guys. I actually do not have a set list of how my husband should act, look, or anything of that nature. I hope he will have the character traits I mentioned earlier, but I entrust all of that to the Lord. I've come to realize that He knows what I want and need far better than I do.

I do not, by any means, suggest we create checklists and quickly dismiss all guys who don't satisfy those lists. I do suggest we not rush to declare someone as *the one* solely because he displays a few good surface qualities. I have met several guys who appeal to me at the surface level. But upon getting to know them better, I discovered they may not be God's best for me, which is why I have not married any of them.

Just this past weekend, a guy shared his feelings with me. In a nutshell, I told him I needed time to get to know him better (which, to me, involves actually talking, not only texting). You and I should give ourselves time to observe what lies deeper within guys. If the Lord gives us rapid discernment, and if He confirms to us that a guy is the one, then we can certainly and swiftly make that move. We can never go wrong when we follow the Lord's lead. But let's be certain it is truly the Lord leading and not ourselves or others.

Let's not settle for decent, when we serve a God who can do exceedingly and abundantly beyond all we ask or think (Ephesians 3:20). Let's not settle for *good enough*, when we serve a *more than enough* God. Let's not settle due to bleak statistics, when we serve a God who can make all things possible. Let's not settle for the good, when we can have the best.

Faith Walkers

I want to encourage you, my friend, and let you know that I'm on this journey with you. I currently believe all of this by faith. I am single, and I am not having sex. And I pray God has a mate for me who will change both of those facts one day! I am flawed, and I get weak. So I depend on God to help me prepare, dress, and behave as a luxury lady, as a queen. I am trusting in the Lord that if I continue to walk on His path for me, He will lead my king to me at His appointed time. I also trust that He will help me hold it together in the meantime.

That's my encouragement to you. The Bible teaches us to walk by faith and not by sight (2 Corinthians 5:7). That's excellent advice, because if we trust in only what we see, it can be depressing sometimes. We may look around at many of today's guys and think, *I'm not sure there are any good guys, much less God's best guys!* But when we walk by faith, we don't rely on what we do or don't see—we rely on God.

Some people will lead you to believe no godly guys exist, but they do. Other people will lead you to believe God doesn't have good plans for your life, but He does. And His timing is always perfect. So in our journey of singleness, let's be faith walkers and not sight walkers. We may have to remind ourselves to do this many, many times. I know I do!

While we walk by faith, let's learn to be satisfied in our current single season of life, so we can maximize it. Then we will be able to better enjoy our married season of life. If we are miserable single ladies, we will be miserable married ladies. But if we are content while single, we likely will be content while married. Let's be faith walkers now, so we will be faith walkers then.

Reflection Questions:

Think about your current level of modesty and boundaries. Are you more like a Bentley Continental or more like a Kia Rio right now? Explain.

If you think you're more like a Kia Rio, what changes can you make to become a luxury lady?

What are some characteristics you hope for in a mate? Do you have those qualities?

What are some areas of your life that you can work on while you're single and waiting on God's best?

Prayer Starter:

Dear God,

Thank You for accepting me just as I am. Please help me remember that I should seek to please You and not other people. Give me the strength and the courage to remain obedient to You, even when it's not popular. I'd rather be eternally pleasing to You than temporarily pleasing to others. In Jesus' name, Amen.

Section Three

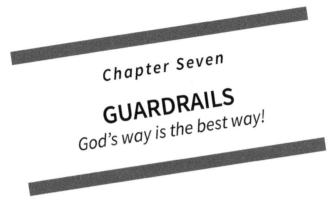

Chapter Seven

GUARDRAILS
God's way is the best way!

"He has made everything beautiful in its time."
Ecclesiastes 3:11

They're Good For You

H ave you ever seen those guardrails on the road? Cities put guardrails in place to keep people from driving off roads, possibly falling from great heights, and seriously harming or killing themselves. I've never heard anyone say, "Those darn guardrails on the road cramp all my fun! If I want to drive off a cliff, that's my business!" If we did hear someone say that, we would probably look at that person like he was crazy. Why? Because most of us understand that those guardrails are in place to protect us, not to ruin our fun.

I do hear people complain about God's boundaries for sex, though. Yet, just like those guardrails, God's boundaries are intended to protect us. What is He trying to protect us from? Well, we don't have to look far in our society to see all the harmful consequences of sex outside of God's guardrails. It causes spiritual harm, emotional harm, mental harm, and physical harm. More specifically, it can cause guilt, depression, self-hatred, STDs, HIV/AIDS, unwanted pregnancies, and a number of other painful circumstances.

God created boundaries for sex to protect us from all of that, but some people make it seem as though He just doesn't want us to enjoy sex. Let's think back to the guardrails along roads. Do they impede drivers' progress to their desired destination? No, they simply guide drivers along the road to their destination safely. Likewise, God did not institute guardrails for sex to keep us from the desired destination (enjoying sex), but rather to get us there safely.

Unnatural Pain

One of the greatest pains I hear people speak of is the pain of breaking up with a lover. Why does that pain cut so deeply? When people's bodies attach during sexual intimacy, their emotions and souls attach too. As a result, a part of them remains endeared and attached to each other, even after they physically break up. That causes the heart deep, deep pain.

This kind of pain is unnatural, because God never intended for our hearts to feel that particular pain. Whether we live sexually pure or not, we will all experience *some* pain on this earth. But we were not meant to experience *that* one. God intended sex to be for married, life-long partners, with death being the only condition for a "break up."

At some point in your life, you may have heard the phrase "consummate the marriage." Basically, that phrase means that a marriage becomes *official* only after the couple has sex. While the marriage licenses, the wedding ceremonies, and the name changes all have their place, sexual intercourse is what truly finalizes a marriage in the eyes of God.

So when people go around having sex with several different people, they are, in a sense, *marrying* all of those different people. That's why the separation hurts so badly, especially for ladies. Whether we're aware of it or not, whenever we sleep with someone, our bodies, hearts, and souls attach to that person as our life partner. And if that person leaves us and *marries* other people, it causes an unspeakable, unnatural pain. God never wanted us to feel that pain.

Yet, due to His abounding love, grace, mercy, and forgiveness, God can heal, restore, and redeem us from that severe pain. So if you have experienced, or if you are currently experiencing that pain, be encouraged, my sister! Take your broken heart to our Almighty God in prayer, and let Him mend it. It will take time, but if you fully give your heart to God, He can and will heal it.

If you have not experienced that pain, I plead with you to avoid ever experiencing it. I know some ladies say that they can sleep around with guys and feel nothing; they say they can do whatever guys do. I know other ladies say abstinence is old-fashioned and having sex is no big deal. But these ladies are lying to themselves, and they are lying to you. As far as you can help it, don't go down that unnaturally painful road.

Packing Light

When you prepare to travel, are you a light packer or a heavy packer? I must confess that when I travel, I pack *a lot* of stuff. I like to have plenty of outfit options, so I pack far more clothes and shoes than I actually need. As a result, my suitcases can become quite heavy, and I struggle to move them from place to place. Thank God for those handy wheels on the bottom, or I wouldn't get anywhere!

However, I have the *complete* opposite approach when it comes to my heart's emotional baggage. In that respect, I desire to pack as lightly as possible. I don't want to collect any unnecessary or extra emotional baggage before uniting with my husband. Can I enter my marriage with no baggage? Not a chance. Why? Because as I mentioned earlier, we cannot avoid all trouble in this life.

In the Bible, Jesus tells us that we *will* have trouble in this world (John 16:33). He does not say, "it's likely" or "maybe." He says "will." That declaration lets us know we cannot avoid all problems. We are born with some issues, such as a dysfunctional family or a hereditary disorder. We also get some issues through others' bad choices, such as the harmful effects of being abused or abandoned. However, we bring some problems on ourselves through our own bad decisions. The emotional baggage we pick up due to premarital sex belongs to that last group of problems. I aim to minimize those kinds of problems in my life. I pray you will do the same.

I think of it this way: Imagine the Lord has allotted me 80 pounds worth of burdens to bear during my time on this earth. Well, since there's no way to avoid them, I want to carry *only* those 80 pounds and nothing else. I don't want to have sex with someone outside of marriage and pick up 15 more pounds, sleep with someone else and pick up 15 more pounds, give in to an addiction and pick up 10 more pounds, and so on. No, thank you! I'll stick with the 80.

You and I know pain isn't measured in pounds, so the numbers I've used are random. I've simply used them to illustrate a distinction between life's unavoidable troubles and the extra ones we bring on ourselves. I don't need any *extra* trouble in my life. How about you? If you and I know we'll experience trouble in this life, why in the world would we go out looking for more trouble to add to it? Sounds crazy, huh? Yet, that's exactly what we do when we ignore God's guardrails for sex.

I encourage you to think about that before you give your body to anyone outside of marriage. A few moments of pleasure can cause a lifetime of pain, and temporary happiness can cause permanent consequences. Ask yourself, *Is this worth the extra baggage I'll have to carry when this is over?* And I pray you will conclude, as I have, that the answer is "no."

It may be helpful for us to consider the following questions as well: *How many people do I want to "marry" before I actually get married? How many additional people do I want to carry into my marriage?* Personally, I don't want my past to weigh down my future. I want to pack light. How about you?

Extra Baggage?

What if you've made some sexual purity mistakes in the past? What if you've already picked up extra baggage? Should you just keep on doing it, since you've already started? No ma'am, not at all! As long as you're alive, it's never too late to commit or recommit your life to Jesus Christ. The Bible tells us that God's mercies are new every morning (Lamentations 3:23). You can start over at any time. You can start over right now!

Plus, if you simply keep doing what you've been doing, you'll only add on more weight. So let's imagine you've picked up an extra 10 pounds of emotional baggage. Wouldn't you prefer to stop there rather than adding 10 more pounds on to that? 10 pounds weigh less than 20, 20 pounds weigh less than 30, 30 pounds weigh less than 40, and you get the picture.

Don't dig a deeper hole for yourself, my friend. Drop that shovel! Then start praying for and working toward your deliverance. We cannot change our past actions, but we can change our present and future ones. We can decide that from this day forward, we will do things God's way.

It's Better His Way

I really love all fruit, but I especially love yellow apples. I had a big craving for a yellow apple one particular day, so I went to the kitchen to get one. Yet, to my dismay, I discovered that all the yellow apples looked more green than yellow. None of them had fully ripened yet. I wanted one so badly, though, and I wanted it right then! So I grabbed one, washed it off, and ate it.

It didn't taste terrible. You could even say I enjoyed it. However, as I chewed, I couldn't help but think about the fully ripened yellow apples I had eaten in the past. They tasted so much sweeter than this one, and I enjoyed them so much more. This un-ripened yellow apple was okay, but those ripened ones were much better.

I began to feel some regret. *Why didn't I just use some self-control?* If only I had waited until the apple was ready. If only I had waited for the right time to eat it. I would have enjoyed the experience so much more.

Guess what, my friend? This same principle applies to sex. Sure, we *can* have sex outside of marriage, and we could probably find some momentary enjoyment in doing so. But afterward, when we realized that we had cheated ourselves out of God's best, we would surely regret it. Yet, if we will just wait for the right time for sex—God's time—we will enjoy it so much more. It may seem good the world's way, but it's much better God's way.

You may be thinking, *But Leah, people make it look and sound so great. They say there's nothing better.* Well, those people may truly believe there's nothing better than premarital sex, but it's because that's the only way they've had it. I would have thought that an un-ripened apple was the best if I had not eaten a fully ripened apple beforehand. I would not have known there was something so much better.

Whose opinion should we trust more anyway, the worldly people's or God's? Let's imagine you just bought a new curling iron for your hair, but you don't know exactly how to use it. Whose opinion will be more valuable to you, your friend who just bought one too and is equally as confused as you, or the person who created the curling iron? If we want to know how to use something, the best person to ask is its creator.

God created sex, not these people in our world. His opinion on sex is the best one. If you used that curling iron the way your friend told you and ignored what its creator suggested, you could do some serious damage to your hair. And you may even have to walk around with that awful burnt-hair smell! Likewise, if you take this world's opinion on sex and ignore God's, you will do some serious damage to your life. So let's trust the Creator. He knows best.

Many people having sex the world's way will try to convince us that we're missing out. But they're truly the ones missing out. They're missing out on the joy and the blessings of doing things God's way.

A New Look at "Missing Out"

I must admit that at points in my life, I felt as though I was missing out. As I mentioned in "Victoria Not-So-Secret," I would observe the clothing and behavior of my university's most popular ladies. Many of them made it seem like having sex outside of marriage was no big deal. In fact, they made it seem normal. They all dressed a certain way, went to all the clubs and parties, and were casually having sex.

Praying to God simply means communicating or having a conversation with Him, and we don't always need to kneel down and talk out loud to do it. So as I walked to my dorm room one day, I prayed in my heart saying, "God, I feel like I'm missing out. I'm looking at all these other ladies, and to be honest, it looks like I'm missing out on what they have." In true conversations, we not only speak, but we also listen. When I listened that day, do you know what the Lord allowed me to realize? He helped me see that I was exactly right. I truly was missing out.

In fact, I was missing out on a *whole lot*. I was missing out on the broken fellowship with God that sexual sin can cause. I was missing out on the guilt and shame that often follow sexual sin. I was missing out on the mental and emotional pain of breaking up with a sexual partner. I was missing out on crying myself to sleep after a lover failed to acknowledge me in front of his friends or told his friends about his sexual experiences with me. I was missing out on urgent, panic-filled trips to the local clinic. I was missing out on HIV, AIDS, and all the STDs. I was missing out on pregnancies out of wedlock. I was missing out on disappointing my parents, my family, and all the little girls looking up to me.

Yeah, I realized I was "missing out" alright. And the more I began to think about all I'd missed out on, the more I began to rejoice in utter gratefulness to God. I began to pray again, but this time I said, "Thank You, God, for everything You've allowed me to miss out on! Please allow me to continue missing out on any and everything that's not of You!" You see, I wasn't missing anything the Lord didn't want me to miss. And if you do things His way, neither will you.

I pray that you and more young ladies will miss out on the trash this world offers. If we have to miss out on something, let's miss out on sin and unnecessary troubles. Let's miss out on the world's momentary pleasures that never satisfy and gain God's eternal joys that never disappoint. Let's miss out on the world's way, and do things God's way. I'm going to stay within God's guardrails for sex. How about you?

Reflection Questions:

How do you view God's boundaries for sex now?

How might staying within God's boundaries benefit your life?

Prayer Starter:

Dear God,

Thank You for the guardrails You have put in place for sex. I know You have put them in place to protect me. Please forgive me for the times I have flirted with or stepped beyond Your boundaries for sex. Help me rest in Your protection and not fight it. Please give me the wisdom and the strength to stay within Your guardrails for sex and live sexually pure. In Jesus' name, Amen.

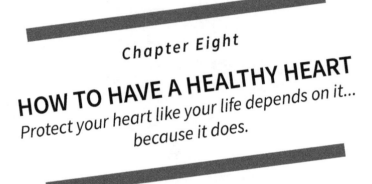

Chapter Eight

HOW TO HAVE A HEALTHY HEART

*Protect your heart like your life depends on it...
because it does.*

"Above all else, guard your heart, for it is the wellspring of life."
Proverbs 4:23

Heart Check

How can you ensure you have a healthy heart? I'm not referring to your physical heart health but your emotional heart health. In order to ensure we have good emotional heart health, we must guard our hearts. As we do for our bodies, we must put boundaries in place for our hearts. We must be very careful about what and who we allow to enter our hearts. This is critical, because everything we are and everything we do flows from them (Proverbs 4:23). Our thoughts, words, and actions all reflect the makeup of our hearts.

It's also important to realize that our hearts and bodies are closely linked. Once something or someone has accessed our hearts, it's much more likely that same something or someone will access our bodies. So, if we don't guard one, it will be difficult, if not impossible, to guard the other. It is for this reason that boundaries for our hearts are just as vital as boundaries for our bodies.

Don't Fall Too Soon

Let's be honest, my friend. Some of us ladies are just *in love* with the thought of being *in love*. I'm not saying you are, but I'm sure you know someone who is. I don't think there's anything wrong with having a romantic side, but we must be careful with this whole *falling in love* thing. That very phrase, "falling in love," can be misleading.

If you or I were to trip over a rock and fall into a ditch, I'm certain we would do so unintentionally and involuntarily. I mean, maybe it's just me, but I would never *choose* to trip over something and fall into anything. Yet, when we fall in love with people, it is not like accidentally falling into a ditch. We don't do it unintentionally or involuntarily. To the contrary, we *choose* to love people. Our attraction to some guys may be involuntary, but loving them is totally up to us.

We should be careful not to confuse infatuation or admiration with love. The mere facts that we're attracted to a particular guy and enjoy his company do not mean we love him. They simply mean we're attracted to that particular guy and enjoy his company. Over our lifetimes, we will meet many guys who are attractive and fun to be around. If that's how we define love, we will *fall in love* every other week!

How can we not fall in love too soon? Well, for starters, we should be careful not to let guys we just met occupy our minds *all* day every day. (You can use the same strategies we discussed in the Mind section of this book to keep your thoughts on the right track.) We also should be careful not to share deeply personal and intimate details about ourselves so quickly. In fact, I believe there are some things we should share with only our husbands. These are just a couple of examples, but overall, we should seek God before we emotionally attach to any guy.

Falling in love easily and haphazardly poses great danger to our heart health. If we give our hearts away quickly, we run the risk of getting them broken quickly. We should take a step back and realize this truth: There will be several guys we *could* choose to love, but we *should* choose to love only the one God picks.

I'm sure there are plenty of guys I could love as my husband, but I desire to choose the man God has chosen for me. Recognizing that we get to choose who we love allows us to better guard our hearts. We won't open our hearts to every guy with a nice smile and charismatic personality. We'll know that love is not a fleeting feeling but rather a lasting choice.

What Love Looks Like

Love involves the consistent display of selfless and respectful actions over time. Nice words and warm, fuzzy feelings play roles in love, but actions play the lead role. And I believe true love really kicks in when people still *show* love, even when they don't *feel* like it. I won't include a "how to know a man loves you" section in this book, because to be perfectly honest, I don't know if that certain guy loves you. But here's what I do know: God is love (1 John 4:8), and His sacrifice for our sins remains the greatest display of love ever. So, if you want to know what love looks like, I suggest you look to God and His Word.

Count on Accountability

One day in Austin, Texas, I took a stroll with my iPod and new headphones, just bouncing and singing as I walked. I saw the icon that signaled it was my turn to cross the street, so I began to step off the curb. All of a sudden, despite the sound of my music and my own singing, I heard someone shout, "STOP!" I froze, and to my shock, I saw a car speed right through the red light. The car had been outside of my peripheral vision, so I didn't see it coming.

I usually don't appreciate people raising their voices at me. In fact, that's one thing that can get me really upset. But do you think I was angry with that lady for shouting at me before I walked into the street? Not at all! To the contrary, it took everything within me to keep from hugging a complete stranger. Yes, she did yell at me; but she did it because my life was in danger. If she had been "more friendly" about it, I may not have heard her.

Likewise, at times in our lives, we may not see the danger of sexual impurity coming our way. This is why it's good to have a least one person "watching our backs," in a sense. When this person sees our sexual purity may be in danger, she can warn us before we walk into it. In essence, this is accountability. It helps us stay in line as we try to guard our hearts and overall sexual purity.

Need Help Staying in Line?

Let's be honest. If you know someone is watching you, are you more or less likely to do something unethical? I'm guessing less likely. There are a lot of things we don't do that we probably would do, if it weren't for accountability. For instance, I'm sure a lot more people would steal money from their jobs, if they didn't have coworkers, employers, and security cameras holding them accountable. I'm sure a lot more people would skip working out at the gym, if they didn't have friends and personal trainers holding them accountable. When used the right way, accountability can be very beneficial to us in many areas of our lives, especially in this area of sexual purity.

What might sexual purity accountability look like? Well, let's say one of your sexual purity goals is to stop listening to sexually explicit music. Your accountability partner may periodically ask you how you're doing on that goal. The two of you may even look through your iPod together and make some decisions. Or perhaps you meet a guy you really like. Your accountability partner may frequently ask you if you're keeping up your physical and emotional boundaries. Basically, just like other forms of accountability, sexual purity accountability helps reduce your chances of acting inappropriately.

This accountability practice can really help us guard our hearts, so I pray you will consider making it a part of your life. The most important piece is choosing the right partner. The following are a few characteristics to look for.

Good Fruit

If you are serious about your sexual purity and your overall Christian walk, your accountability partner should be a committed Christian. Why did I say *committed* Christian? Are there *uncommitted* Christians? Well, quite frankly, yes. Some people call themselves Christians but do not live as such. I've heard several other terms for people like this—*carnal* Christians, *part-time* Christians, etc.—but the bottom line is that these people talk one way but live another way. We all know the old saying, "Talk is cheap." That saying may be trite, but it's true. 1 John 2:4 reads, "The man who says, 'I know [Jesus],' but does not do what He commands is a liar, and the truth is not in him." I don't need to say anything about that verse. It is abundantly clear!

Committed Christians actually work to live holy and to please God (Romans 12:1). They aim to live in compliance with the life and teachings of Jesus Christ. Does that mean committed Christians are perfect? Not at all. But do they strive for consistent righteousness? Absolutely.

In the end, uncommitted Christians do not strive for consistent righteousness. These people rest comfortably in their lives of sin. We do not want these people as our accountability partners. Thankfully, we can identify both committed and uncommitted Christians by the fruit of their lives (Matthew 12:33). What are examples of their fruit? The words they speak, the health of their relationships, their works for the Lord, and so on. Truly examine the condition of people's lives before you link up with them as accountability partners.

Why is this so important? Well, in order to have a successful accountability partnership, both of you must be aiming at the same target; you must have the same goal. Imagine you're trying to shoot an arrow at a target. Your partner directs you on how to aim and shoot your arrow. Can your partner help you hit the bull's eye, if you're both looking at different targets? I don't think so. I smell failure! And if we partner up with people who don't share our goals, that's exactly how our accountability relationship will end—in failure. So let's choose partners who share our godly goals.

Ladies Only

Another characteristic of effective accountability partners is that they should be our same gender. Yay for the ladies! Allowing guys to be our sexual purity accountability partners could be tricky for obvious reasons. Aside from the sheer awkwardness of sharing sexual purity struggles with guys, doing so could become counterproductive; meaning, it could actually lead us into sexual impurity.

I'll never forget the testimony of a young minister I once heard speak. This young man went to a woman's apartment to pray with her about her sexually promiscuous lifestyle. Yet, after they prayed together, they slept together! The moral of the story is this: Sharing sexual purity struggles with members of the opposite sex poses great, great danger. In our attempts to be sexually pure, let's not walk into obvious sexually impure traps.

I can already hear people saying, "There are exceptions to every rule, Leah!" I bet there's even a woman who claims to have a great sexual purity accountability partner of the opposite sex. If that's the case, then

I'm very happy for her. But as for me, I don't intend to ever seek out guys as my sexual purity accountability partners. I believe my good friend, Wisdom, agrees with me on this issue. I hope you will too.

Take It Like a Woman

We should seek out accountability partners who are not only committed Christians and females, but who will also tell us the truth. Just like the lady who warned me about the oncoming car, they should be more concerned about being honest with us than with making us feel good about ourselves. If our accountability partners just want to make us happy all the time, they won't be very helpful to us.

When discussing the importance of accountability to sexually-pure living, my dear friend, Dr. Stephen Trammell, highlighted the accountability relationship between David and Nathan in the Bible. (Notice that they were both guys!) David fell deeply into sexual sin. Nathan sternly confronted David about his sexual sin and even raised his voice to him at one point (2 Samuel 12:1-14). Keep in mind that David was the king, the main man, the head honcho! But did David's position cause Nathan to hold back any punches? Nope. He hit David with the ugly truth right between the eyes.

Likewise, when our accountability partners see we're in danger, they should be willing and able to do what Nathan did for David—tell us the truth regardless of how uncomfortable or hurtful it may be at the moment. We may not like it, but we will appreciate it.

Put It In God's Hands

Accountability is key, but the very best way we can guard our hearts is to place them in God's hands. Let's fall head-over-hills in love with Jesus before falling head-over-hills in love with a guy. Doing so does not mean we will never get disappointed or hurt in a relationship with someone. Whenever we deal with humans, some disappointment and pain come along with it. But when we hide our hearts in God's hands, we gain access to His wisdom and protection.

If we utilize that wisdom and rest in that protection, we can avoid allowing predators (guys who intend to harm or use us) into our hearts. If we don't use our God-given wisdom or embrace His protection, we leave our hearts open to harmful invasions. So let's not go that route, my friend. Let's entrust our hearts to the Lord and use practical strategies, such as not falling in love too soon and teaming up with an accountability partner. If we take these steps, we will do wonders for our heart health. Share that with your doctor during your next checkup!

Reflection Questions:

Have you been falling in love too soon in your relationships with guys? If so, how has that affected your heart health?

What's something you can start doing now to better protect your heart?

Who's someone you can start praying about to be your accountability partner? Why do you think she would be a good accountability partner?

Prayer Starter:

Dear God,

Thank You for Your love and protection of me. Please help me use wisdom in how I handle my heart. I desire to entrust my heart to only You. Please don't allow anyone or anything to enter my heart without Your approval. Let me hide my heart in You. In Jesus' name, Amen.

Chapter Nine

DATING GAME
Don't date with only the fun in mind; date with the future in mind!

*"He who walks with the wise grows wise,
but a companion of fools suffers harm."*
Proverbs 13:20

"The Dating Game" was a television show that aired from the mid 1960s until the 1980s. The show consisted of a bachelorette interviewing three bachelors. Based on their responses, she would finally choose one guy to date. It was indeed a dating *game*. Yet, when I observe the state of real-life dating in our society, it appears to be a big game too.

For many, dating has become a mere recreational activity, lacking any intention or purpose. It is this lack of intention and purpose that makes dating's potential harm so great. There's a familiar but insightful quote that states, "When we don't know the purpose of something, we will inevitably abuse it." Witnessing the dysfunction of many dating and sexual relationships today confirms that observation.

So what might purposeful, intentional dating look like? Well, that's precisely what this chapter will explore. It is, by no means, a comprehensive "how-to" on dating. That would be a whole book in itself. Rather, this is an overview of what dating with purpose looks like, and how doing so has been beneficial to me.

What's The Point?

Are you a hard worker? I *can be* a hard worker. In order for me to work hard, though, I have to be able to answer this question: What's the point? If I don't know the answer to that question, I probably will not work hard. I believe working hard without a purpose would be a waste of my energy and my time. And today, that's exactly what many people do in their dating relationships—waste their energy and their time.

Before dating, we should ask ourselves the question I just mentioned, "What's the point?" For some people, the point is just to have fun. For others, the point is to escape feeling lonely or unloved. I'm sure people date for a number of other misguided reasons as well. But as Christians, our ultimate goal of dating should be a Christ-centered marriage.

Have you ever heard a young lady say, "My goal is for a man to break into my heart, play with my emotions, string me along, and never make a commitment to me"? I sure haven't! Yet, that is exactly what's happening to more young ladies than I can count. That's not what they want, though. That's not what any of us wants. We want a healthy marriage, a Christ-centered marriage.

If we have pointless, unhealthy dating relationships, should we expect to reach a meaningful, healthy marriage? If we don't practice Christ-centered dating, should we expect to enjoy a Christ-centered marriage? Keeping these questions in mind will prove to be helpful in our dating relationships. What's the point of dating to you? It's very important that you and I can answer this question and answer it well.

The figure below is an illustration of how intentional dating relationships may progress. We've established that a Christ-centered marriage is the center, so let's briefly work our way out.

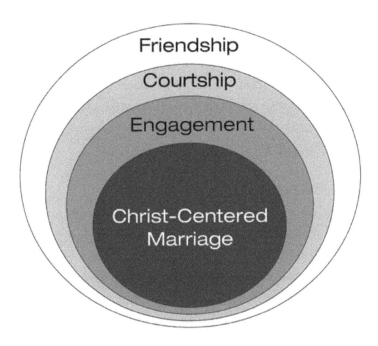

Developed by Laura Gallier Ministries, lauragallier.com.

Fully Engaged

The engagement phase is the "prep zone" for marriage. Basically, couples prepare spiritually, mentally, and practically to be together for the rest of their lives. We can relax our emotional boundaries a bit in this phase. By this point, we should be confident this is the person God has chosen for us. However, because it is not official until we say "I do," I don't recommend we completely take down our hearts' boundaries. I believe that, like my body, a part of my heart should be reserved for only my husband. And *almost* married is not married.

It is for precisely that reason we should not relax our physical boundaries *at all* during this engagement phase. In fact, it may be wise to increase our physical boundaries during this phase. The hurricane danger alert levels range from categories 1 to 5. As hurricanes get closer to land and wind speeds increase, their danger levels increase. Likewise, as we get closer to guys emotionally, our purity danger alert levels should increase. Stronger emotional attachments can cause stronger sexual temptations. Since the emotional bond should be quite strong by the time we reach the engagement stage, our purity danger alert level should probably be a Category 5! Let's just be careful not to get too cozy, too soon.

Get To Know Him

Before engagement, there can be a courtship phase. I've heard different definitions of the term "courtship." When I say courtship, I mean a time of exclusive dating in order to get to know someone better. We can use this time to verify if the guy truly is who we hope he is. We should heavily guard both our hearts and bodies in this stage. Not doing so can cloud our better judgment. It can cause us to ignore obvious signs that a guy is not who we hoped he was.

Sometimes, we mistake mutual attraction for love and compatibility. That's one reason it's so dangerous to relax our emotional and physical boundaries too early. It would be quite hurtful to get deeply involved in a relationship, only to discover that love and compatibility never existed in that relationship.

I know a young lady who met a guy she really liked. After dating a while, she and the guy became sexually active and moved in with one another. Things seemed just peachy for a little while, but then she started to see the *real* guy. She found out he had a pornography addiction, he was verbally abusive, and he had absolutely no intention of ever marrying her. Whoa—talk about a letdown.

Needless to say, this young lady really wants to break up with her boyfriend. Yet, since she has had sex with him, and since he pays half of her rent, she feels as though she literally cannot break up with him. She got in too deeply before verifying his true nature. This happened due to many mistakes on her part, but especially due to her sleeping and living with the guy outside of marriage. Acting married while we are single is the quickest way to get in too deep, too early.

The lesson I take from her story is *don't skip the courtship phase*. We should protect our hearts and bodies, and truly get to know the person. After asking God to show us that person's true character and waiting long enough to see it, we can make much more informed decisions. Doing so can spare us a lot of drama and some extra pounds of baggage.

Boys Who Are Friends

My dad was not a fan of the *boyfriend* idea when I was a teenager. He would say, "Leah, it's better to have 'boys who are friends' than 'boyfriends'." I think, yet again, Daddy "O" was on to something. We should actually place great value on genuine friendships with guys. Aside from the worth of good friends in general, having guy friends is a good way to see characteristics you may like or dislike in a mate, without having to date a ton of different guys.

There are two things I should mention, though: First, let's resist the urge to view every nice guy we meet as a potential mate. This practice is emotionally unhealthy, and it can cause us to appear desperate (which isn't a good look, by the way). It can also ruin potentially good friendships before they even begin.

Second, when I say genuine friendships, that's exactly what I mean— genuine *friendships*. Let's be careful to be friendly and not flirty. The line between friendly and flirty may be thin, but there is indeed a line. We should never seek to give guys false hope or play with their emotions. That behavior is not becoming of a lady and certainly not of a Christian.

Also, if we make a habit of playing that game, it won't be long before we get beaten at our own game. The Bible tells us that we get out of life what we put in it (Galatians 6:7). So if we put out a lot of empty flirting, that's what we should expect to get in return—emptiness. But if we put out genuine friendship, I believe the Lord will bless us with some genuine friends in return. In this friendship phase, it's best to keep it light, keep it fun, and keep praying to the Lord for guidance. I'd like to share a bit more of my journey with you now.

My Teenage "Love" Affair

As I mentioned, my father was not a fan of the whole dating idea, and thus my "love life" didn't really exist in middle school and high school. In retrospect, I'm actually grateful for that. Since I didn't get involved in any of those soap opera-like teenage romances, I found great success in school. I did what I was in school to do—learn! As a result, I was admitted to all the universities to which I applied and attended my dream university (Go Longhorns!).

If you are currently in school, let my testimony encourage you. Stay focused on your primary purpose for being there, which should be to graduate. And if you're wired like me, it should be to graduate with honors! Even if we don't particularly like school, we are called to do everything like we're doing it for God Himself (Colossians 3:23).

If you're in middle school or high school, it's probably best to stay in the friendship phase with guys. If the purpose of dating is a Christ-centered marriage, is there any reason to seriously date at this point? I don't have anything against those teenage crushes, talking on the phone and texting, going to prom, and all that stuff. I'm just pointing out the uselessness of those serious teenage relationships that cause young ladies to lose their focus in school.

One day, my Grandma Josie said, "Leah, focus on your education right now. Guys aren't going anywhere!" And guess what, my friend? Grandma was right. I graduated at the top, and guys are still around today. Go figure!

College Guys

My academics remained my primary focus in college, but I must admit, I was excited about meeting some college guys. During my first semester, a guy from one of my classes asked if I'd grab a bite to eat with him on campus. I agreed, and we had a nice time. But after that one outing together, this guy concluded I was *the one*. He constantly called me to the extent that I couldn't receive any other calls, and he began to exhibit stalker-like behavior.

This experience totally freaked me out. After the situation got resolved, by none other than the Lord and my dad, I avoided close relationships with guys and dating for a while. I didn't want to hear anything any guy had to say! That reaction was probably a bit extreme, but since God works all things together for our good, it was quite beneficial to my academic success.

Then, along came my *dream guy*. I met him my junior year, and I thought he was amazing. He loved the Lord, he was cute, he was funny, he was cute, he worked hard, and did I mention he was cute? In reality, he and I were in the friendship stage, but in my heart and mind, I carried us into the courtship, engagement, and marriage stages. I envisioned our beautiful wedding and our adorable children, and I thought my first name coupled with his last name was a match made in Heaven!

However, it turned out that Heaven had nothing to do with my plans. It was *all* me. So when that guy's path and mine went in separate directions, it hurt me. I learned a valuable lesson, though: Never let my emotions get ahead of God. Verifying our emotions with the Lord's will remains the best way to guard our hearts.

Lesson Learned

A couple of years later, I remembered that lesson when a guy asked my dad for permission to date and eventually marry me. He and I had known each other for a little while, and we were attracted to each other. I thought it seemed like a fairy tale, and I was excited. Even so, I was careful to keep my emotions in check.

As we spent more time together, I naturally formed an emotional bond with him. Yet, the strength of that bond was limited, because I did not share my body or the intimate parts of my heart with him. When we talked, I would share some details about myself, but I never opened my heart to him.

As much as I really did want to believe he was the one, and as much as I really did want to be in love, I just couldn't do it. Even though this guy and others talked about how good we looked together, and that we were sure to get married, I just couldn't drop my heart's boundaries.

My lesson from the past taught me to always check with the Lord before I release my heart to someone. And the Lord did give me confirmation about this guy. He confirmed the guy was *not* His best for me at that time. Part of me wanted to look past the signs and stay with him. *Maybe he'll get better*, I thought to myself. Then, I thought about this quote from Maya Angelou: "When people show you who they are, believe them." When guys show us their true character, it would be unwise for us to ignore what we've seen.

I knew the relationship needed to end, but I dreaded the detachment process. Due to the amount of time we spent together and our mutual friends, the detachment was difficult. It hurt too. You may be thinking, *But wait, Leah, didn't you say you guarded your heart and body?* Yes. *And the breakup still hurt?* Yes. So can you imagine how much more difficult and hurtful it would have been, if I had given him my heart and my body? It would have been immensely more painful. It would have been much harder to let go.

Not having physical and emotional boundaries causes many ladies to stay in unhealthy relationships. The strong emotional and physical bond they feel keeps them from leaving. I'm not claiming I handled everything perfectly in my relationship with this guy, because I didn't. He and I probably should've spent more time in the genuine friendship stage and spent less time alone. However, I was able to let go much more easily than I would've been able to, had I not set physical and emotional boundaries.

Is Dating Bad?

I want to make it clear that I don't believe dating is bad. I believe dating with no or wrong purpose is bad. When done God's way, I believe dating can actually be beneficial. Because of that relationship I just shared with you, I gained more knowledge and understanding about God, myself, and what to look for in a mate. And since I protected my virtue, I didn't lose much of anything. This is the beauty of protecting our hearts and bodies in dating relationships—we gain much without losing much.

I do not believe many women can say the same about their relationships, and that hurts my heart. I don't like to see ladies lose themselves in relationships. I'm praying many young ladies will read this book and be inspired to hide their hearts within the Lord's loving hands. I pray we won't share our hearts or bodies with anyone of whom He does not approve.

So, Why Are You Still Single?

It happened again. While engaged in a great conversation about life and ministry, one of my peers asked, "So, why are you still single?" I suppose that question is a compliment. It seems that what the asker is really saying is, "Based on what I've seen and heard from you, I believe you'd make a good spouse, so what's the hold up?" And it seems the further we progress through our twenties, thirties, and beyond, the more curious people become about what's "holding us up" from getting married.

As a follower of Jesus Christ, I believe that He is in complete control of my life. I believe He orders my steps and brings things to pass in my life in His perfect timing. (I do have to remind myself of these truths on occasion, though.) Thus, as I tried to conjure up a grand answer to why I'm single, I reached this simple reality: I'm single, because God has not led me to marry anyone yet.

I know, I know, that sounds so *spiritual*. But as Christians, life works best for us when we allow God to take the lead, especially regarding marriage. In fact, after the decision to accept Christ as our Savior, I believe the marriage decision is the most important one. Trust me, my friend, it would behoove us to let God lead us into our marriages, not those other leaders. *What other leaders?* I'm so glad you asked!

The Ticking-Clock Leader

I've known that some people think they should be married by a certain age. I never thought I was one of those people, though, until two weeks before my 25th birthday. I took a mental inventory of all the single guys who had expressed an interest in me, and I realized something: I wasn't willing to marry *any* of them. So, not only would I not be married by age 25, I wouldn't even *know* anyone I would marry! Oh. My. Goodness. I felt the panic rising within me, right up until God reminded me that our numerical ages mean very little to Him.

The Bible tells us that our measure of time is not the same as God's measure (2 Peter 3:8). We are constricted by time and space, but He is not. He sees the end from the beginning and can easily move in, out, and beyond our time. Therefore, if He has spouses for us, He will bring them at His appointed time. Yes, we can rush ahead of God and get married on our time, but we will also face the consequences. For instance, I could rush and get married at 25, but then I could also be perpetually miserable and possibly divorced by 28. My encouragement to you and myself is this: Let's allow God to be our leader, not our perception of time.

The Loneliness Leader

Some people let loneliness lead them into relationships and marriage. But marriage is not a cure for loneliness, and thus there are a number of married, lonely people. Besides, if we allow loneliness to lead us into a relationship, how will we know that we truly desire to be with *that* person? We won't. I'm sure we all experience lonely moments, and I'm sure many of us desire companionship. It's okay to acknowledge those feelings, but it's not okay to follow them.

Although easier said than done, we singles must learn to practice the presence of God and allow Him to satisfy our hearts. His Word promises that He will always be with us and that He is enough for us to be content (Hebrews 13:5). Also, even if we do marry the people God ordained for us to be with, they will not be able to satisfy *all* our needs *all* the time. After all, they will be flawed, limited people, just like us. So finding satisfaction in God alone will not only benefit our singleness, but it will also benefit our marriages (if marriage is in God's will for our lives).

The Lust Leader

As we've discussed, most of us have sexual desires, and those desires aren't inherently sinful. Sexual lust, on the other hand, is a problem. The Apostle Paul actually does advise singles that it's better to marry than burn with lust (1 Corinthians 7:9). However, if you read that entire Scripture, you'll quickly see that Paul did not think that was the best option. As usual, I agree with Paul for many reasons, but I'll briefly share two.

First, marriage will not cure an overall issue with lust. If we frequently lust after people while we're single, we'll continue to lust after others when we're married. That's a heart issue, not a marital status issue. So, I strongly encourage that sexual strongholds—lust, porn addictions, etc.—get rectified during your singleness.

Second, sex alone is a terrible reason to get married. Two of my dear friends recently got married, and they both told me they're glad they didn't expect sex to be like it's portrayed in the movies. (Just so you know, it's *not* like the movies.) Yet, sex within a marriage is beautiful, because that's the context for which God designed it. But sex should not be what leads us into a marriage. God should lead.

God Can Handle Your Love Life

If you and I are Christians, that means we believe God can handle our eternal souls. If we believe His Word, that means we believe He can handle creating the universe, parting seas, slaying giants, healing the blind, and resurrecting the dead. If we believe He *can* handle all that, does it really make sense to believe He *can't* handle our love lives? I don't think so. So, in this dance of love and marriage, let's allow God to take the lead, and let's kiss those other leaders goodbye.

What Do We Do Now?

So what do we do while we're single and waiting on God's mates for us? Our singleness provides us with the best opportunity to pursue God fully. During this time, He's the only one we should try to please. Before moving on, there are two more things I'd like to briefly highlight about singleness.

First, singleness is not an inferior way of life. I believe the Apostle Paul would agree. In fact, Paul asserted that the single way of life is the better way (1 Corinthians 7:8). It is likely that he never got married. And let's not forget that the greatest person to ever walk the earth, Jesus Christ, never got married either. Don't get me wrong, I believe marriage is a beautiful, beautiful entity, and I do pray it's in God's plans for me. I simply want us to be careful not to over glamorize our future marriages and thus undervalue our current singleness.

The second thing I'd like to point out about singleness is that it's a time of great freedom! Since we tend to have more flexibility in our schedules, we can serve more, travel more, explore more, and generally just do more than people with family obligations.

The most significant freedom, though, is that of our hearts and emotions. Many singles often forfeit their freedom when they try to act married before actually being married. When was the last time you intentionally tried to get arrested and put in prison? My guess is never. You enjoy your freedom and wouldn't purposely exchange it for bondage. That would be crazy. Yet, that's exactly what single ladies do when they give their hearts and bodies to men who aren't their husbands—they exchange freedom for bondage. So let's not go there, my friend. Let's enjoy this singleness freedom while we have it.

Now, back to that opening question. What do we do while we're single and waiting on God's mates for us? *We chase God's purposes for our lives, and we live to His glory!* This is much easier to type and read than it is to actually do, but it's our goal nonetheless.

Notice that I said pursue *God's purposes*, not pursue guys. I know our society glorifies that overly-aggressive woman persona, but in reality, it's not a good look. That aggression quickly begins to look like desperation or promiscuity, neither of which becomes a luxury lady. We should aggressively pursue God, period. Doing so will enable us to see God, ourselves, and our purposes more clearly. It will also help us see guys more clearly.

Also notice that I did not say we should sit around waiting for our mates to find and pursue us. Instead, we should *pursue* God and *live* to His glory. Those are action words! Yes, we're waiting for God to bless us with mates, but waiting does not mean sitting idle. Waiting, in itself, does not help us grow in our relationship with the Lord; *how* we wait does. So let's be productive in our singleness. As we discussed in the "Bentley Continental vs. Kia Rio" chapter, let's focus on becoming queens and let God handle the arrival of our kings.

A New Attitude

In a few months, I will be a bridesmaid in my god-sister Erica's wedding. Let me give you her stats: She's 31, she's a doctor, and she's a virgin. Do you think she has been productive in her singleness? She certainly has. Even so, she'll be the first to tell you that her wait has not been easy. She's proof that successful waiting is possible, though. And I'll let you in on a secret, my friend: Her story happens more often than you may think. So learn to be satisfied and productive in your singleness and hang in there! Like my god-sister, you'll be glad you did.

Take a look at what my good friend Chere once wrote: "When it comes down to it, I really don't mind waiting on my mate. I have a really good life serving God and His people, although I admit I take that for granted sometimes. But who knows, if I am supposed to settle down with someone, this process just means God is grooming me more. So, if or when He brings me a groom, the only thing I'll need to say is 'I do!'"

I really like Chere's attitude! She points out that, in reality, waiting for God to bless us with mates is not as dreadful as people try to make us believe. Being single is not the end of the world. It can be difficult, but it can be great too. If we focus only on the difficulties, we can lose sight of the great joy and advantages singleness allows, especially in regards to serving the Lord.

For me, it's a daily process of renewing or making over my mind. Singleness challenges me, but I desperately yearn to maximize this season of my life. I believe the Lord will honor my desire. If you desire for Him to make you whole in the midst of your singleness, I believe He'll honor yours too. No person can complete us. Only God can do that.

Notice that my friend Chere said, "If or when He brings me a groom." Here's a somewhat uncomfortable truth for us, my friend: Not everyone will get married. That's all the more reason we should seek our fulfillment in Christ alone. God may call some people to lives of singleness, and that is a noble call. That being said, it doesn't seem as though He calls most people to lives of singleness. While some people will never get married, many people will.

So if you and I can just get lost in the Lord, it's likely we'll find ourselves walking down the aisle one day. Let's do as my friend says and allow the Lord to groom us for marriage during our singleness, so we will indeed be prepared for our grooms.

The Takeaway

The dating relationship model I presented in this chapter does not represent the "commandments of dating." You don't have to follow these stages, and not following them doesn't necessarily mean you won't have a Christ-centered marriage. That said, it is definitely a sound, biblically-based model of how intentional dating progresses, and I do believe following it would benefit your life.

The primary points I want you to take away from this chapter, though, are the importance of intentional dating and the importance of contentment during singleness. The alternatives are hazardous to our heart health and to our overall sexual purity. If there's no point to it, don't do it! Ask God for wisdom about how to navigate relationships with the opposite sex and follow His directions.

Reflection Questions:

What did you think dating's purpose was? What do you believe its purpose is now?

Do you see any benefits to following this dating model, or at least dating with a clear purpose?

What can you do to help yourself stay free and satisfied during your singleness?

Prayer Starter:

Dear God,

Thank You for Your perfect plan and timing for my life. Please give me wisdom regarding whom I decide to date. Please help me guard my heart against those who intend to hurt me. Even though I may long for a companion at times, give me the strength to be content while I'm single. When a guy comes along of whom You approve, please give me clarity and peace, so I'll know he's the one. In Jesus' name, Amen.

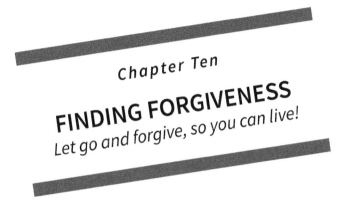

Chapter Ten

FINDING FORGIVENESS
Let go and forgive, so you can live!

"Forgive, and you will be forgiven."
Luke 6:37b

It's Not Over

As you've been reading this book, you may have felt tinges of guilt and shame. Perhaps you've thought about your past sexual sins, or even your current sexual struggles. You may think my story sounds great, but that it can't apply to you. I'd like to begin this chapter with a brief interview I had with a young lady. Maybe you will find some similarities between your story and hers.

Q: How old were you when you lost your virginity?

A: I lost my virginity at the age of 14. I found myself in a relationship with my first boyfriend. It was not something that happened on its own. In fact, we both planned it beforehand.

Q: Why did you make the decision to start having sex?

A: I began engaging in sexual activity due to personal issues I did not know how to deal with. To me, sex was a way out of feeling worthless, unloved, and unappreciated. Growing up, I did not have the opportunity to witness what "love" was. My parents consistently argued. They were not able to display love to me very well. My mother suffered from different addictions, so I never was able to construct a relationship with her. My father was always at work, which prevented me from having a relationship with him too. I felt alone and unloved, so I would find myself clinging to the idea of sex. I had the mindset of, *If only I could find someone to just touch me or caress me for the night, someone to just show me some type of affection, that would be all the "love" I need.* In other words, I was looking for love in all the wrong places.

Q: How did having sex before marriage affect you?

A: For me, I believe the biggest effect of having sex before marriage was bondage. I allowed myself to become bound to all the wrong people for all the wrong reasons. With girls, sex isn't just sex; it creates feelings you might not have even known you had. By having sex before marriage, I found myself having many feelings for many people, which led to my self-destruction. Sex before marriage also made it hard for me to remain abstinent after the first time. After the first time, I thought to myself, *Well, I already committed the sin, so I might as well proceed with it, if it ever comes up again.*

Q: When did you decide to live sexually pure for Christ?

A: I believe I decided to live sexually pure after hearing a sermon from my pastor, Pastor Mike, during his "Single & Free" sermon series. By listening to this sermon, I was able to learn that an external solution does not solve an internal problem. Sex was the source of A LOT of my problems. In order for me to get all areas in my life straight, I had to restrain myself from sex. I'm so thankful to Pastor Mike!

Q: What have been the effects of living sexually pure?

A: Living sexually pure has done more for me than words can explain. By living sexually pure you begin to learn a lot about yourself. You also learn how to love and appreciate yourself for who you are. Sex creates bondage, and we all know bondage creates distractions. Living sexually pure has allowed me to get myself back on track and let a lot of unnecessary things go. A lot of women suffer from low self-esteem or battle with the feeling of unworthiness. Living sexually impure only adds more fuel to that fire. It all starts and ends with committing yourself to God. Living sexually pure opens doors!

Maybe your story is not exactly like this young lady's, but you may have started having sex at a young age for reasons similar to hers. Now, you may feel as though your mistakes disqualify you from this sexual purity journey. You may think it's all over for you. Well I have news for you, my friend: Your past mistakes DON'T disqualify you, and IT'S NOT OVER for you!

Every day we wake up, we get a new chance to lead a sexually pure life. Remember, the Bible tells us that God's mercies are new every morning (Lamentations 3:23). That doesn't mean we should intentionally fall short one day, knowing that we can just start over the next day. But it does mean we should not let one day's failure rob us of the next day's victory.

Excessive guilt and unforgiveness are not of God. So, like sexual impurity, they do not belong in our hearts. In order to keep them from trespassing in our hearts, we must forgive ourselves and others. Let's take a closer look at why we should and how we can forgive.

Drop That Stone

We should forgive ourselves and others because ultimately, we *all* make mistakes. Our missteps may take different forms, but they are missteps nonetheless. Some of our past mistakes resulted from a lack of knowledge; we just didn't fully know what we were doing. In other instances, we knew what we were doing but didn't fully understand the consequences of doing it. And then there are some of us who both knew and understood our actions but decided to rebel. Whatever the case, God always sees something worth redeeming in us. Even the deepest, darkest sinful places are within the territory of God's love and forgiveness. No matter how far you've departed from God's plan, you're still within His reach.

One time, Jesus stopped the stoning of an adulterous woman with one comment: "If any one of you is without sin, let him be the first to throw a stone at her" (John 8:7). One by one, people dropped their stones and walked away. Why? Because we all make mistakes! The Bible says that *all* have sinned and fall short of God's glory (Romans 3:23). I'd like to mention that Jesus truly was without sin, so technically, He *could* have thrown a stone at the woman—but He didn't. He had already forgiven her. Since God forgives us, we should forgive ourselves. Then, we should extend that same forgiveness to others. It's much easier said than done, but I've noticed that most worthwhile things in this life aren't particularly easy.

Get Up and Get Moving

If we fall into sexual sin, the quicker we repent to God and forgive ourselves, the better. Be careful not to wallow in failures. Do not fall into the "Well, I've already messed up, so I might as well keep on doing it" trap. That logic may seem to make sense in the moment, but it really doesn't.

If you fell onto the street and a car ran over your leg, would you then say to yourself, "Oh well, I already have an injured leg, so I might as well just stay here on this street"? I don't think so! I think you would try to use your *one* good leg and roll or hop your way off that street!

The same principle applies to all sin but especially sexual sin. If we fall, we need to actively and quickly work toward getting up. The longer we stay in it, the more difficult it becomes to get out of it; and the longer it takes us to get out of it, the more severe the consequences. For us to get the victory, we must quickly get up from our failures and get moving toward the Lord. We won't be able to do that, though, until we forgive ourselves.

Forgiving ourselves doesn't mean we're excusing ourselves from our sins. It means we have acknowledged our wrongs, made peace with God through repentance, and decided to move forward from our failures. To the contrary, unforgiveness and condemnation paralyze us, or worse, cause us to regress. They make us feel as though we cannot approach God, and that we're not worthy to live out His callings on our lives. But these are lies, my friend.

God always has open arms into which we can run. No, we are not worthy to live out His callings on our lives, but He makes us worthy! So if you've fallen into sexual sin, and if you've been camping out there for a while, I encourage you to make a move. Repent to the Lord, forgive yourself, take practical steps to avoid making the same mistakes, and look ahead. Get up and get moving!

When We Stumble

Do you like to watch the Olympic Games? I sure do. I've noticed that in many of the sports, such as track & field, ice skating, and gymnastics, there's a difference between *falling* and *stumbling*. If an athlete falls in one of those events, she receives major deductions on her score, and she may even automatically fall out of medal contention. If she only stumbles, she will still receive score deductions, but they won't be nearly as severe; she can still win a medal. Clearly, there's a difference between falling and stumbling.

Sometimes we may not downright fall into sexual sin, such as become addicted to pornography or have sex outside of marriage. However, we may experience sexual purity stumbles at times—situations in which we come close to falling. For example, I had a really tough time keeping my thoughts pure one particular night. I had gone to the movies with my family that afternoon. While the movie was fairly decent, many of the previews leading up to the movie were not. My attempts to look away came a bit too late, and consequently, some sexual innuendos and images found their way into my eyes and ears. I felt pretty good right after we left the theatre, though. I thought, *Yes, I dodged those bullets!*

Yet, when all the day's noises and lights faded, and I was left with only my thoughts, I realized some bullets actually did hit me. Remember those battles between the ears we discussed earlier? Well, let's just say I fought in a heated battle that night! Each time I captured one thought, another one came along. I woke up the next morning feeling somewhat discouraged and saddened that I had struggled so much. *Why did I agree to go to that movie? Why didn't I close my eyes sooner? Why did it require so much effort for me to stop those thoughts and throw them out?*

I felt really bad until I remembered something: We cannot walk through this life or this sexual purity journey with perfection. We strive for perfection, but we will inevitably stumble from time to time. The way we respond to our stumbles is crucial, though. In fact, our response to stumbles will determine our ultimate success. A mishandled stumble can lead to a destructive fall. Conversely, a well-handled stumble can lead to a stronger dedication to live victoriously!

Take my experience as an example. If we have a rough night like I had and decide to sulk over it for a while, we may become so discouraged that we stop fighting for our minds. We may begin to let those thoughts have their way, and thus we may spiral into a sexually impure stronghold, such as a sex addiction or pornography addiction.

On the other hand, if we repent to the Lord quickly and ask Him for guidance, we will become encouraged. We may even feel more determined to live holy and pure lives. Maybe we'll decide not to attend movies of a certain rating or not to watch the previews before the movie or to stop going to the movies altogether. Maybe we'll begin to explore less risky forms of entertainment and discover something we really enjoy. These two responses to stumbles hold vastly different outcomes. Personally, I prefer the latter scenario—the one in which we repent quickly and move on with greater determination to live sexually pure!

Just Ask Paul

If there was an official "Followers of Christ Hall of Fame," the Apostle Paul would have to be on that list. Yet, even the great Paul admitted that he had not arrived at perfection; but he was pressing toward that perfection (Philippians 3:14). In the meantime, Paul didn't beat himself up over his failures. He decided to forget the past and look forward to the future (Philippians 3:13). We should do the same thing!

When we ask God for His forgiveness, He gives it to us (1 John 1:9). His forgiveness doesn't provide a "keep on sinning" pass, but it does give us a "get out of guilt" pass. So we must accept God's forgiveness, forgive ourselves, leave the past behind us, and walk toward the future with great expectations. Beating ourselves up will only delay our progress and diminish our power. If Paul had done that, he would not have accomplished God's great plans for his life. And that would've been tragic, because he wrote nearly half of the Bible's New Testament and helped spread the Gospel throughout the world!

God has great plans for you and me too. And in order to reach His greatness for us, we must resolve to forgive ourselves and keep moving forward. I'm moving forward, my friend. Will you join me?

Pass It On

Once we've enjoyed the sweet forgiveness of the Lord, we should pass that forgiveness on to others (Ephesians 4:32). When we forgive others, it actually benefits us more than the person we've forgiven. It frees us from bitterness and anger and allows us to truly move on with our lives. It would be nice to receive an apology, but we should not depend on that. Waiting for them to apologize before we forgive supplies them with the power. Choosing to forgive them regardless of what they do gives us the power.

Forgiving others can be quite difficult, especially in regards to sexual sins. In some situations, reaching a place of forgiveness may even require additional resources. For instance, if you've been sexually abused or sexually assaulted, it may be beneficial to seek professional, Christ-centered counseling. The percentage of females who have been molested or sexually assaulted in their lifetimes is staggeringly high. If you can find a support group in a local church or Christian program, that could be helpful. You may find the encouragement from ladies who've had similar experiences to be especially healing.

I also recommend looking into the story of Bridget Kelly as featured in the TAASA's "Speak Up. Speak Out." ads. Her testimony of how the Lord brought something so beautiful out of such an ugly situation truly inspired and touched me. I pray it will do the same for you, especially if you've endured a similar circumstance. For additional help in healing from sexual abuse or trauma, you may consider various organizations, such as Joyful Heart Foundation, Christian Survivors, or any other trustworthy programs.

I pray for healing and deliverance in your life, my sister. I pray you will find forgiveness—forgiveness from God, forgiveness for yourself, and forgiveness toward others. Let's forgive, so we can live.

Reflection Questions:

Have you been allowing some of your past mistakes to keep you from moving on? If so, how has that impacted your life?

How might accepting God's forgiveness benefit your life?

How might forgiving someone who hurt you benefit your life?

Prayer Starter:

Dear God,

Thank You for being faithful to forgive me when I fall. Please help me to forgive myself and others as well. I desire to release any unforgiveness, bitterness, hate, guilt, shame, or condemnation within my heart. Please take it, Lord. Please set me free. In Jesus' name, Amen.

THE "NO TRESPASSING" PLEDGE

I pledge to boldly look sexual impurity in its face and declare, "Enough is enough! You will not trespass in my mind, you will not trespass on my body, and you will not trespass in my heart. I am God's property, and I will live for Him."

_____

Signature

_____

Accountability Partner Signature

_____

Date

A NOTE FROM DADDY "O"

To all of the young ladies who have read *No Trespassing: I'm God's Property,*

The Bible says that you are *wonderfully made* (Psalm 139). You are so precious and special to God, because you are made in *His Image, His Likeness.* Therefore, I encourage you to avoid settling for less than God's best for your life. Do not rush into relationships with young men, because it appears that everyone else has a boyfriend or because young men find you attractive.

Please don't allow your self-esteem to be based on men's view of you. Do not engage in relationships where you have a "partial" commitment. Know this: When the LORD blesses you at *His* appointed time, He will bless you with 100% of a man, who will love Him first and be totally committed to you second. All the LORD asks of you is to simply have faith and trust in Him and Him alone! God bless you!

—Daddy "O"

MOST IMPORTANT RELATIONSHIP

Perhaps as you read this book, you decided you'd like to have a relationship with the true and loving God of whom I speak. Or maybe you've accepted Christ as your Savior but would like to recommit your life to Him. Whatever the case, you can benefit from reading through this overview of how to be saved.

In order to be saved, you must...

- **Recognize and admit that you are a sinner.**
  "For all have sinned and fall short of the glory of God."
  Romans 3:23
- **Know that you deserve to die for your sins.**
  "The wages of sin is death..." Romans 6:23a
- **Understand that Jesus died in your place.**
  "God demonstrates His own love for us, in that while we were yet sinners Christ died for us!" Romans 5:8

- **Ask God to forgive you for your sins and receive His free gift of living forever with Him.**

  "...But the gift of God is eternal life through Jesus Christ our Lord." Romans 6:23b

- **Say with your mouth that Jesus is Lord and believe in your heart that He defeated death.**

  "If you declare with your mouth, 'Jesus is Lord,' and believe in your heart that God raised him from the dead, you will be saved. For it is with your heart that you believe and are justified, and it is with your mouth that you profess your faith and are saved." Romans 10:9–10

You may want to pray this prayer:

Dear Lord Jesus, I know that I am a sinner. I recognize that You are God's Son and that You died on the cross for my sins. I confess my sins before You and by faith, I receive Your gift of eternal life. Thank You for saving me. In Jesus' name, Amen.

Next Steps:

Once you accept or recommit to Christ as your Lord and Savior, I suggest three things:

- Get involved in a church that places Jesus above everyone and everything else, including the pastor, money, and material things.
- Find a Bible study plan that works for you.
- Pray, pray, and pray some more!

TESTIMONIALS & REVIEWS

This book touched me as well as made a lot of things clear to me. I struggled in many areas of my life and reading this book put me back where I needed to be which is in God's Path. Great book and POWERFUL BOOK! I finished the book in less than a week. Every female should read!!! Loved it.

—**Rosetta**

While today's young ladies are drowning in confusion about their self-worth, dating, sexuality, and romance, Leah Holder Green comes alongside readers like a sister and sheds lights on CRUCIAL truths that today's young women absolutely need to know. The book is not preachy; it's inspiring - not a long list of "dos" and "don'ts" but down-to-earth advice about how to avoid common sex-related pitfalls and pave the way for lasting romance. Great for parent-teen discussions and small group gatherings.

—**Laura**

I wanted to read a book on abstinence and after watching Leah Holder Green's video on YouTube, I found her opinions on the subject very unique and inspiring. I'm glad I purchased her book. It was very easy to read and she gave a lot of practical tips that people can easily apply to their lives to stay physically and spiritually pure. Although, this book is mostly directed at females, I think guys can also learn a lot from this book.

—Danny

From reading *No Trespassing: I'm God's Property*, I learned how much control I have over sexual temptation and my sexual purity. Leah Holder Green's advice is very practical and not "preachy." This is a spiritual, mental, physical, and emotional handbook, and I highly recommend it to all young ladies!

—Kelly

What a blessing *No Trespassing: I'm God's Property* has been. I couldn't put it down! Leah Holder Green is such an inspiration and wise beyond her years. I'll be 40 years old this year and have lived a celibate life since the death of my husband in 2005. Life is sometimes challenging. I know Leah may have written this book with the teenagers and single young adults in mind, but she touched my heart and spoke to it so candidly. She reminded me of my self-worth and how important it is for my physical and spiritual health to be virtuous. Lining up with God's word is truly a blessing.

My daughter (age 14) is enjoying the book as well. She's been sharing it with her friends over lunch. Leah speaks her language too, and she's getting a kick out of the humor Leah uses. I am grateful for this book!"

—TJ

Mrs. Leah Holder Green empowers young women with the truth about sexual purity. Although sexual purity is a topic that most people shy away from, Leah has taken charge and she has chosen to speak openly and candidly about the complexity and simplicity of sexual purity.

—Kristine

This is a gem of a book and an essential item in the library of every single woman of any age. Leah Holder Green pours out the heart of God on every page of this book. There is such a need for righteousness to be spoken into the lives of women who have to grow up in a sex-driven society such as the one we live in. I recommend this book to parents, uncles, aunts, Godparents, etc. Gift this to the young woman of your life and suggest that she save her "gift" for the one that God has set aside to bless her with as a husband.

—Vincent

It was extremely refreshing to encounter this book. These days, many young people are more focused on keeping up with their peers and doing whatever they want, without considering how patience and self-control will pay itself off in unimaginable ways in the future. Just when the world started painting purity as weird or overrated, this book came along to assure us that purity is good, it should be strived for and it was God wants from us. Thanks Leah!

—Jasmine

OMG! *No Trespassing: I'm God's Property* has been such a blessing to my life. I promise the way I think and act have tremendously transformed—especially on what I listen to and what I allow myself to watch. *No Trespassing* has also allowed me to grow in my relationship with God, and I feel myself becoming closer and closer to Him every day. Thank you, Leah, for reaching out and sharing your testimony!

—**Simone**

Reading this book is like having a heart-to-heart conversation with a close friend. In this book, I found advice, encouragement, and even a little reproof regarding things that I've taken too lightly. It is a book that I'll likely read again and again, just to keep reminding myself of my commitment to sexual purity and find encouragement for staying the course. I'm almost 27, and I've had my share of struggles, but I am in it to win it! Our bodies are temples of the Holy Spirit, and this book contains a message that this current generation really needs to hear. Stop reading this review and start reading this book if you haven't already!

—**Divine**

This book is absolutely wonderful! I want every girl to read it and be blessed by it. Leah Holder Green does such a great job of lovingly connecting truth about sexual purity into modern teenage vernacular. She provides sound logic and strong Biblical application. She goes to the heart of sexual purity issues with such stark honesty and clarity that every teenager and adult can relate to and be benefited by this book. *No Trespassing: I'm God's Property* is a must-read for teenagers and young adult women!

—**Dr. Mark Hartman**

Where was this book when I was a teenager? Leah communicates encouraging, straight-forward truths about sex and relationships at a time when our culture desperately needs to hear it. This is a must-read for every teen girl and young woman, as well as single adult ladies.

The truths in this book not only have the power to change lives but to transform our society.

—**Laura Gallier**

Leah Holder Green has mounted a frontal charge on the issue facing every single person in America today—whether or not to have sex before marriage. She has given straight talk about this sensitive subject and laid a foundation that every single person in America can build on. Though not excluding any individuals, her focus on youth in the dating years of their lives is both refreshing and compelling. Read this book to gain insight into how you can counsel others. Apply these principles that she has so clearly stated and you will find the blessings of God upon your life. This book is a must-read for every single person in America today!

—**Jimmy Draper**

NOTES

NOTES

NOTES

NOTES

CPSIA information can be obtained
at www.ICGtesting.com
Printed in the USA
LVHW04s0917110818
586658LV00001B/12/P

9 781630 473693